Up from the Soles of Our Feet

A Woman's Reader

Kristin Palm, Colleen Reader, Susan Paurazas,
Denise Thomas, Suzanne Dolan Manji,
Nancy J. Henderson, Barbara Shooltz Kendzierski,
Stephanie Matthews and Donna Stubak

Edited by Margo LaGattuta

Plain View Press
P. O. 33311
Austin, TX 78764
512-441-2452

http://www.eden.com/~sbpvp
e-mail: sbpvp@eden.com

The cover assemblage, The Duende Chair, © 1997, was created by
Suzanne Dolan Manji. The objects were chosen for their
relationship to the images in the writings throughout the book. The
open head of the female symbolizes the collective voice of women.
Art in the Heidelberg Project, located in Detroit, was created by
Tyree Guyton.

Acknowledgments:

The authors wish to acknowledge prior publication of (or awards
for) the following pieces which appear in this book: "Air-Ride
Equipped," **Suburban Lifestyles**, © 1997 Margo LaGattuta;
"Abstract Art," First Place Library Award from the Milford Fine
Arts Association, 1997, Colleen Reader; "it's just a phase,"
Speakeasy, © February 1996, Denise Thomas, also published in **A
Wise Woman's Garden**, May 1996; "I Told Him My Name Was
Lola," **Lunch**, Vol. I, No. II, © 1995 Stephanie Matthews;
"Riverwalking," **Lunch,** Vol. I, No.3 © 1996, Stephanie Matthews.

Contents

Foreword   7

    Air-Ride Equipped   9

Relativity   11
Kristin Palm
    Solstice   11
    Wifey   12
    Nearer, Still Nearer   14
    Super Mean   16
    Poem for Pode   17
    Nice Rack   19
    Motor City Trilogy   24
    Relativity   30
    Lunar   31

Some Days Begin at my Toes   33
Colleen Reader
    Abstract Art   33
    Fruit with Still Life   34
    Fringe   35
    Cocktail Hour   36
    Staying Up Past My Bedtime   37
    Modus Operandi   38
    Nighttide   39
    Losing the Familiar   40
    Watchmaker's Wife   42
    Adirondack Chair   45
    Jesus Upon His Retirement   46
    Hands   48
    Full Circle   50
    Stereoscope   53

Delicacy   55
Susan Paurazas
    Uncharted Waters   55
    Being Herd   56
    Laundry Day   57
    Sestina: Summer   58
    The Kiss   60
    Delicacy   61
    Secret Recipe   62
    The Scent of Granny's Roses   64
    Month of Sundays   66
    Angels in the Snow   68
    Perennial   69
    Quiet Midnight   70
    Reunion   71

Purple Haze   72
A Lot of Little Things 74
Leaving Chance   75
Each Small Choice   76
Standing on the Edge   77

A Guide to the Modern Life 79
Denise Thomas
Illuminations for the Practicing Poet   79
A Guide to the Modern Life   80
Night Blindness   80
Requiem   81
(*Gazing through Veils*)   83
Sense Assault (Urban) 85
Sleeping in August   86
Titus Andronicus redux 87
Bioadhesive Carnal Pharmaceutica   89
Cartography   91
It's Just a Phase . . .   93
Nodding Beauty   94
Notes for An Informal Study of the Personalities of Tables   100
Botany Lesson   101

Close to the Bone   103
Suzanne Dolan Manji
The Opthamology Lesson   103
Close to the Bone   106
Nabeel   108
Roots and Wings   111
Don't Go . . . Don't Stay   120

The Millionth Snowflake   123
Nancy J. Henderson
Some Thoughts on How I Write 123
The Photographer   124
Moving   126
Relying on Intuition and the Millionth Snowflake   127
Since You Left for Ruidoso   128
All the Gray   129
Repacking my Bags   130
Parity   131
Letter to a Friend   132
Reading   134
Fog   135
Getting On With It   136
Re-creating   137
Daylilies   139
Starting Out 140
Unveiled   141
Down Deep 142

Uprising   145
Barbara Shooltz Kendzierski

Uprising   145
My Sons   146
Walking the Dog   147
Soul Garden   148
The Little Engine That Could   149
Laundry Lesson   150
Summa Cum Laude   151
Driving Blind   152
Death Interrupted   154
Saturnalia   155
By Design   156
Duet with my Grandmother   158
Postcard from the Lobby of Detroit Receiving Hospital   162
Born of Night   164

Living by Definition   167
Stephanie Matthews

Nature's Revision   167
Riverwalking   168
The Cabins on Chief Lake, Norwalk, Michigan   170
Spooning   172
The Spoons that Feed Us   174
Working Eulogy   175
Pandora's Box   177
Searching for what I Believe   180
Painting Spaces   181
Universal Prescription: Desire   182
Learning by Definition   183
I Told Him my Name was Lola   184
Men for Sale   186
Before Letting Go   187

Last Days of a Life Under Cover   189
Donna Stubak

Last Days of a Life Under Cover   189
Riding Shotgun for the Ragman   190
The Crucifixion of Rabbit   193
Fuzzy White Edges   194
Petey-bird   196
Tap Dancin' for Rita Bell at the Red House Chinese Restaurant   197
The Revolving Door   199
Playing Chicken   201
Tea Time   204
Mom Makes Production on the Midnight Shift   206
Little Elevations   207
Rose Monday   209

About the Writers   215
Contributors' Notes   218

If I read a book and it makes my whole body so cold no fire can ever warm me, I know that is poetry. If I feel physically as if the top of my head were taken off, I know that is poetry.

—Emily Dickinson

Foreword

Margo LaGattuta

    The well-known poet and artist Federico Garcia Lorca coined the term *duende*, which is a Spanish word for *ghost*, to signify the struggle artists go through in the creative process to transcend the power of darkness in the soul. In his essay *The Duende: Theory and Divertissement*, Lorca spoke of language that emerges "not from the throat, but up from the very soles of the feet." This is a poetry that is rooted in place, in the heart of each writer's landscape (both inner and outer), and emerges with a force that is both explosive and true.

    The stories and poems in *Up from the Soles of Our Feet* come from such an honesty. The nine Michigan women writers, Kristin Palm, Colleen Reader, Susan Paurazas, Denise Thomas, Suzanne Dolan Manji, Nancy J. Henderson, Barbara Shooltz Kendzierski, Stephanie Matthews, and Donna Stubak, met for a year in my dining room to collaborate and create this book. It is the third Michigan collection I have edited for Plain View Press in Austin, Texas, and is part of a national series of regional anthologies called New Voices. The first two are *Variations on the Ordinary* and *Almost Touching*.

    Here are the voices of women who speak the truths of their lives, who dare to discover and celebrate that which is dazzling, ordinary and unsung. And their work grows from the very fiber of Michigan landscape: driving a car in the Motor City, remembering the Rag-man in Hamtramck, honoring a mother who worked on the line at Chrysler, taking a night walk along the Manistee River, visiting cabins on Chief Lake, writing postcards from the lobby of Detroit Receiving Hospital, watching a sunrise over Lake Huron, surviving the assault of urban living, mourning over lunch in Charlie's Crab. The authors emerge from various backgrounds: attorney, dentist, visual artist, nurse, engineer, writer, as well as wife, mother, daughter, grandmother.

There is magic in these pages, as the women transform suffering and loss into a triumph of the spirit. There is surrealism, humor and the probing of inner landscapes. Each voice is unique, yet together they raise a collective voice of intensity, grace and burning curiosity that is Woman at her creative best.

I include one piece of my own, an essay that appeared as a column in *Suburban Lifestyles* newspaper in Rochester, Michigan. It speaks to the power of landscape in our lives and to the spirit of renewal.

Air-Ride Equipped

It must be summer, because I'm driving I-75 north to Gaylord again. And I feel that old freedom gathering in my heart, that joy of leaving it all behind one more time, as I drive right up into the sky, up up over the Zilwaukee Bridge, onward through hordes of Winnebagos and station wagons with trail bikes and silver canoes on their roofs, through potholes the size of Rhode Island from last winter's ice storms.

Onward and upward I fly, like the crows, past rest stops and outlet shopping malls with special weekender discounts, up through vistas of white birch and evergreen, over the hills, watching my speed as the holiday cops peer out from bushes at hidden highway turnarounds, past Jeeps carrying boats with names like *Fancy Free* and *Our Escape*, and I wonder what we're all escaping out here on a highway headed right up the middle of a mitten. What stresses have we left behind, as we head for bear and wolverine country, and how can nature cure us, refresh and renew us for the long slide back down on Sunday evening?

This time a stop in Traverse City brings back memories of an earlier life, my lingering in the mist over Leelanau, and (yes, it's really true) a sport-capped bottle of natural spring water called *Leelanau Mist* purchased at Horizons bookstore. Who would have thought humans would one day purchase plain water with a fancy name for a buck and think they were drinking-in the horizon? And, yes, I fall for it, taste that sky blue pink mist over the harbor at Leelanau and quench my thirst for sunsets and early morning seascapes. As the label on the water bottle reminds me, *Leelanau* is a Chippewa Indian word meaning *delight of life*, and I realize that is what I'm seeking each year on my various treks to places magical at the peak of my state.

I have to go up higher to see it, get out of my daily shoes and put on my wing-tipped fliers to delight in the ordinary again. To view anew—perhaps with many of the same people who ride bumper-to-bumper in their azure cars along Telegraph Road down below—a sky full of eager stars and a lingering moon. And hope we can all bring that life back home with us on Monday morning.

© 1997 Margo LaGattuta

Relativity

Kristin Palm

Solstice

There is a lifting.
It has so little to do with the heat
of the sun and so much
to do with the clarity
of the moon, the sopping
smell of earth and bark and blossom,
the hidden crickets' steady pizzicato,
the undertow of freshwater waves
we feel in hollow spaces,
the ever-pressing desire to climb
into it, pull ourselves closer,
awake with it, breathe deeply,
as if to suck in the sky,
etch this season in the core
of our bones, release

and watch it rise.

Kristin Palm

Wifey

It's on days like this,
when the last bus has left
me at curbside to breathe
Detroit's gray and gravely air,
when one too many shirtless
man has asked me for a dollar
or at least a piece of ass,
when all I want is to get home,
pick my dirty underwear
off the bathroom floor and shove
two weeks of trash in the pantry
before company claims the futon
for the weekend,
that I think I could settle
with you.

We'd buy a lakeside
suburban bungalow
3 bdrm, 2-1/2 bath,
1-1/2 gar, bsmt,
fireplace, ctrl air, great
location, close to schools
neatly trimmed lawn, neighbors
who build decks and expand
driveways, chauffeur kids
in mini-vans to hockey or rehab,
wave when we meet
at the corner and talk
behind our backs.
I could own a Crockpot
and a Cuisinart, puree my way
around your heart.

We'd raise children on reading,
writing and Ritalin,
teach them *No means no,*
D.A.R.E. to keep them off drugs,
brag on bumpers that they
are Students of the Month,
congratulate ourselves for caring
enough to monitor cable.

We could take walks,
limit our cholesterol,
grow old healthy and happy
with high returns and low handicaps,
sleep safe and secure,
having invested in our future.

You would hold me in your arms
at night and I would nestle close,
whisper in your good ear:
Is this love? Or just the slow
sloughing off of my soul?

Kristin Palm

Nearer, Still Nearer

I know that my Redeemer lives.
What comfort this sweet sentence gives.
He lives, He lives who once was dead;
He lives, my everliving head!
　　　　　　—Christian hymn

She was ready to go
the first time, lay shivering
in the back bedroom,
the one that smelled of lavender,
where I used to sleep and she
used to whisper prayers.

And though we couldn't believe
she would leave us in autumn—
not in the season of dying—
the less devout among us
couldn't take a chance.

We said good-bye one
by one. She kept her face
to the wall and sang parched
hymns, not turning even when
I put my mouth to her ear, whispered
in the language of her childhood,
Jag älskar dej, farmor.
I love you, Grandmother.

But He (the one she believed in)
wouldn't take her. Not yet.
Christmas came and there she was,
a breathing ghost, drinking black coffee
at the kitchen table and saying she remembered
nothing—not the pastor delivering
last rites, not her daughters

reciting *Tryggare Kan Ingen Vara,*
not the crazy cousin repeatedly asking when
we were going to eat—nothing
except that someone had promised
the great-grandchildren would be baptized.

How fitting that she should finally go
at Easter, two years later.
The last time I saw her,
she recognized me only a minute. She
smiled and took my hand, let me brush
her thin, white hair, soft
as lilies in the pulpit, soft
as moss emerging from snow, soft
as her lavender scent.

Super Mean

Katherine decides that we'll be witches for Halloween and we'll wear stupid pointy hats and we'll be super mean. Then she jumps on the bed and insists that for her birthday we'll have a slumber party at my house. She sits on my lap at the adult table and halfway through dinner makes me go with her to the bathroom, where she decides that I should adopt her and that we should live in a mansion. We'll have a swimming pool as big as her house, and her parents and sisters will be servants. We'll eat dessert first, have salt and sugar for every meal, and for grace we will say, "Tasty!" After dinner we sing about buses and bears and dance around the living room to Blue Mountain and the Grifters. She doesn't leave until midnight. I take off for the bar down the street, where the cute guy from the record store barely looks up long enough to say hi. I drink one beer and leave. There's nobody there to play with.

The next day, Katherine invites me over so we can run around in our underwear. When I tell her to ask her parents, she says she killed them with a jar of poison, then asks what would happen if she stuck a knife in someone's heart. I run these statements by my own mother, the teacher and consummate answerer of questions, whose most memorable lessons to me were to not wear the same bra two days in a row and to remember that a preposition is anything you can do to a mountain. She says Katherine is too young to understand that death is permanent and she watches too many cartoons.

The last week in October, Katherine decides she doesn't really want to be a witch. Meghan will be a baby and Andrea, a princess, but Katherine isn't divulging her plans. On Halloween night, we bundle up and wait at the foot of the stairs. Katherine is taking forever. Andrea won't wear her princess coat and puts a parka over her dress. Meghan wears the black lipstick I brought for my witch costume. She is a very creepy baby. We yell for Katherine to hurry up. A door slams upstairs and Katherine descends, smiling sweetly, dressed as an angel.

Poem for Pode

Kristin Palm

Your coming out
raises some questions.
Not *how could this happen
to such a nice boy?*
(I never thought of you
as a nice boy) or
what about that girlfriend?
or anything else
I know you're afraid
your parents will ask.

For me, along with *what's it like,
are you careful,* and *does he dig
the Velvet Underground,* comes *why
was I the last to know?*

Of course, two years' separation
can fuel doubt,
and there's only so much one can fit
into covert phone calls
where the office foots the bill.
Some things are better said
in privacy and in person.

You played it pretty smooth
by showing me a picture
of the two of you
in Santa Cruz.

It didn't shock me
as much as you had thought,
and certainly not as much
as you had hoped.
I never cared who
you slept with before.

17

But it isn't just sex.
It's you. As you
as eating peanut butter & jelly,
listening to *Live at Max's*
and watching the sunset
at the Cool View.
You should know
you can tell me anything

as long as you never say
you've stopped listening
to rock & roll.

Kristin Palm

Nice Rack

Lacey Lovejoy was the envy of every girl in the seventh grade for the same reason any seventh-grade girl draws stares of admiration and ire—she had huge knockers. That's really what my brother, Jeff, called them. Knockers. His best friend, Kevin Birgy, referred to them as a rack, as in *nice rack* or *check out the rack on that fire babe*. My brother annoyed me. Kevin Birgy disgusted me.

Having racks that did not brandish us *fire*, but something closer to *flicker*, my best friend, Carmen Shephard, and I used to estimate that Lacey's bra size probably approached the number of the bus that picked us up at the corner of Linwood and Preston at exactly 7:32 every weekday morning—36D. On a particularly mean-spirited day, Carmen told me my bra size probably matched the number of the retard bus—26A. This was why I was extra surprised when, after gym class one day, Lacey looked up from her locker and, easing into a contraption that resembled a life vest, informed me, "You need a bra."

"Excuse me?" I replied, feeling both frightened and flattered.

"You need a bra," Lacey repeated. "Weren't you listening in health class today? Mrs. Ratshead said, 'When your breasts start to bloom, put them in their room.' You're blooming. You need a bra. You're not exactly flat, you know." I thought of that Prell commercial where the blonde girl with the pearly white teeth insists, "Your hair will go from flat to fluffy with Prell."

"Well, I'm not exactly fluffy," I replied.

"What are you doing after orchestra?" Lacey asked, laughing. We had played in the same group for two years and sometimes hung out together after rehearsal. I played violin. Lacey played oboe.

"Nothing, I guess."

"I have to go to Penney's to buy my sister a birthday present. She wants this crappy perfume. Want to come with? We'll find you a bra—for your blossoms." Lacey smirked and poked my arms, which were crossed over my chest.

"I've only got five bucks," I said.

"I've got my mom's credit card. We can charge it, and you can pay her back."

"I'll have to call my mom," I said.

"Well, go call," Lacey prodded. "My mom's picking me up outside Penney's when she gets off work at 5:30. She'll give you a ride home."

I didn't feel like telling my mom what Lacey and I were doing. I was afraid she would get all sappy and start talking about how her little girl was growing up so fast. She used up an entire roll of Polaroid film taking pictures of my brother shaving for the first time and botched half of the shots because she couldn't see through her tears. I honestly had a fleeting vision of her baking a cake shaped like miniature boobs. I told her we were going to play video games.

The two hours until the 3:30 final bell dragged mercilessly. As if the day hadn't been long enough already, Lacey had to stay late after orchestra because she was having trouble with her scales. I knew she must be mad because she didn't even want to be in orchestra anymore.

"Mr. Schoenfield sucks," Lacey hissed when she was finally liberated. "Orchestra is so lame." She wanted to be in band so that she could be a flag girl when she got to high school. She wasn't allowed to change until eighth grade because they needed more oboes in the orchestra.

"Well, maybe he'd let you be a flag girl for the orchestra," I offered.

"Shut up," Lacey replied. "Have you ever noticed how the only people he ever makes stay after are me, Trish Anderson and Kysa Collins—the three biggest chests in our class?"

I scoffed.

"No brag," Lacey continued. "It's just the truth. Have you noticed that?"

"Well, yeah," I answered. "But Kysa sucks. She's been last chair all year."

"True. But Trish and I are alright."

"True. Well, my brother told me Mr. Schoenfield looks down girls' shirts. Maybe you should start wearing turtlenecks."

"Gross!" Lacey grimaced. "Maybe I will."

I doubted Mr. Schoenfield had ever tried to look down my shirt. Score one for small blossoms.

When Lacey and I finally arrived at Penney's, we headed for the cosmetics counter to buy Enjoli for Lacey's sister. We both decided it smelled like Lysol. We were still in our Love's Baby Soft phase, and we weren't even supposed to be wearing that. Then Lacey headed for the Teen Miss department. I tried to explain that I still wore a Girls size 12, but Lacey insisted we'd find something in Teen Miss. I knew better. I had wandered by the department countless times before, sizing up the clothes most of my classmates wore, which I knew wouldn't fit me until I was in high school. After one particularly trying incident when I tried to convince my mother that a pair of Body Lingo jeans looked perfectly fine rolled at the waist and cuffed five times at the ankle, I resigned myself to the sad fact that I would be shopping in stores with growth charts in the dressing room until I was old enough to drive. The saleswoman confirmed my suspicion.

"I'm afraid we don't have anything to fit you, dear, and the selection in Pre-Teen is pretty shabby," she said when Lacey informed her of our mission. "Why don't you try next door at The Cricket's Closet? She's got some excellent training bras." Lacey held back a laugh. "It must be nice to have such a petite frame," the saleswoman sighed as we walked away.

"She's right, you know," Lacey said as we examined two Barbie-shaped mannequins wearing striped cowl-necks and corduroy gauchos.

"I want a pair of those," I said, pointing at Barbie's clogs.

"I think it would be alright to be small," Lacey continued.

"You mean flat," I said.

"No, I don't," Lacey said. "I mean small all over. People stare when you're big."

"Yeah? Well, they don't look at all when you're puny." My cheeks felt hot. "Some ninth grader stepped on me in the hall yesterday. He didn't even say sorry."

"Probably the same guy who called me Jumbo Jugs," Lacey said, tugging at the gauchos.

"No, that was probably my brother," I told her.

The bras at The Cricket's Closet hung on the back wall in boxes, as if they needed to be kept sterile. Across the front of each box were the words *My First Training Bra by Sweet 'n' Spicy*. Each size had its own bright color, making for a garish display of reds, yellows, greens and blues. "What brand is your bra?" I whispered to Lacey.

"Maidenform," Lacey answered.

"I hate this place!" I said, loud enough for the clerk to hear.

"May I help you, girls?" she asked, looking up from a display of miniature girls' underwear, which she would later refer to as *panties*.

"Can we try these on?" Lacey asked, gesturing toward the Sweet 'n' Spicy wall.

"Yes, you may," the clerk answered. "But I'm not sure we have your size, hon."

"Oh, it's not for me. It's for her." Out of the corner of my eye, I saw Lacey point at me as I feigned intense interest in the grinning girl on the front of the Sweet 'n' Spicy box. I wondered if I would be as insanely happy wearing My First Training Bra.

"Oh, right," said the clerk. "Just let me get the tape measure."

I looked up from the box.

"They have to check your size. Like with shoes," Lacey explained.

Within seconds, the clerk had me lassoed around the ribs with the tape measure, declaring me a 28AA. The red box. I grabbed one off the wall and headed for the dressing room.

After about ten minutes, Lacey knocked on the door to see what was taking so long.

"I can't get the stupid thing hooked," I whispered through the door.

"Put it on backwards, hook it in the front and then turn it around and slip your arms through the straps," Lacey said. "And come out and show me when you're done."

"I'm not coming out like this!" I felt stupid enough already.

"Put your shirt back on, idiot."

"Oh."

Lacey and the clerk agreed that the bra "flattered my figure." I knew they were using the term loosely, but convinced myself they were telling the truth since I could find no other justification for wearing something that felt like it was cutting off my circulation. I bought two.

On the way home, Lacey and her mom gave me all kinds of advice on mastering the art of bra-wearing.

"Don't tug at the straps," Lacey offered.

"Sometimes they ride up. Go in the bathroom if you need to pull it down," Mrs. Lovejoy added. "And never wear the same bra two days in a row."

"And watch your back. Guys think it's a hoot to snap your bra strap. And it hurts!" Lacey grimaced. "Oh, yeah. And don't let a guy take it off. Unless he's really cute." Lacey giggled hysterically. She could say things like that in front of her mom. She was the only girl I knew who had already been felt up.

"Don't listen to her," Mrs. Lovejoy said without a hint of disapproval as she pulled into my driveway.

I hid my shopping bag behind my back as I opened the front door, until I realized my parents were at my brother's baseball game. Free to model my new purchase in peace, I grabbed a handful of Hydrox from the pantry and ran upstairs to my room. It was a minute before I noticed the package on the bed. I recognized the bag from The Cricket's Closet, and hoped my mother hadn't bought me another miniature Izod polo. She thought they were "so cute" and insisted on adding another one to my collection every time I asked for a ruffle-front blouse or a silver coil belt. I opened the bag hesitantly and pulled out one of three familiar-looking blue boxes. My mother had taped a note to it:

Sandy:

You are becoming a woman. I thought it was time for you to have these.

Love,
Mom

30A. My mother had always pushed me beyond my limits. I tucked the note inside the cover of my diary and threw the boxes into my bottom dresser drawer on top of my too-big nightgowns and out-of-date hand-me-downs from my brother. All the stuff that I figured I would eventually grow into.

Kristin Palm

Motor City Trilogy

I

Everyone crashes
at some point in this city.
Often, we see it coming.
I watched my accident
in the rear view.
As with most things in life,
the apprehension
far outweighed the impact.

Relief came not
so much from the absence
of injury as the determination
that it was not my fault.
Still, I did not emerge
unscathed.

The car, after all,
had been totaled,
a passing
I could not take lightly.
She was my first.
She had a name.

The adjuster's assessment
rang in my ears
like the hideous crunch
of metal on metal:
Total loss.

Never mind
that I'd paid her off,
that I called her Marge.

Never mind
that she'd seen me through
four apartments, two jobs,
Amy's wedding,
Tecla's funeral.
Total loss.

After the exodus of friends
bound for better positions,
my sister's move to the mountains,
my boyfriend's inevitable decision
to leave me for hockey,
after tenuously coming to terms
with all this newness under my skin,
how could anybody take away
this one, last familiar thing?

II

Her insides
felt so new, stiff,
foreign—an import, a sin
in this city, but all signs
pointed her way.

Our most reliable model,
the salesman said,
noting she was the last
on the lot.
A *wise investment*,
my father said,
insisting he'll worry
less.

He called her Ruby
to ease the transition,
recognizing the importance

of a name, remembering
the Subaru he'd relinquished
twenty years ago and only when
the floorboards wore through.

I sat for a while,
breathing her new car smell,
sterile and adult, calculating
interest rates, considering
options—alloy wheels, cruise
control, security. I keyed
the ignition haltingly,
pulled off the lot
slowly, watching
my father
in the rear view,

shrinking.

III

There are days I own
this fucked-
up,
sprawled-
out
mess,
drive the freeways
end to end
just to feel connected.

I don't need power
steering, power locks,
power windows, power
anything. I know
every Marathon station,
Taco Bell and 7-11

from Detroit to Calumet,
can keep myself fueled,
fed and caffeinated
clear across both peninsulas.
I've got Big Chief, Slot,
Thornetta on the tape deck,
the 16-valve thrill of acceleration,
five speeds, a spare tire,
a clear rear view and no sense
of direction.
I've got all the power
I need.

Other days it's too much,
this crazy, cramped culture,
zipping us down freeways
vital as veins, spindly things,
criss-crossing counties,
linking us in ways
we never touch. No standing
on the bus or squeezing
into subways here—
Jesus, we rarely even walk
to the corner—
just 2.2 million half-ton
capsules cruising highways
as familiar as grandparents,
so integral we name them—
Fisher, Jeffries, Lodge—
memorize each pothole
and speed trap in pathetic attempts
to expedite commutes, reach
wherever we're going
to move on
to the next place
and the next,
always late and never

time to stay, damn
the traffic jam, construction,
anything that slows us down.

We curse
congestion, honk
and gesture, punch
up all-news,
all-sports, all-
oldies all the time, cut
each other off,
whatever we can do
to simulate control.

It's 8 am in the Motor City
and traffic is backed up for miles.

We tune in WJR, WCSX,
WWJ, WJLB, WRIF, WHYT
with AAA and eyes in the sky,
traffic and weather together,
up to the minute and on the :08's.

It's 5 pm in the Motor City
and traffic is backed up for miles.

We live fully equipped
and loaded:
A/C, CD and cell phone,
to make us feel at home;
ABS and all-wheel,
so we think that we can stop;
passive restraint and air bags—
NHTSA approved—

to keep us strapped
and cushioned
when we finally
hit the wall.

It's midnight in the Motor City
and traffic is backed up for miles.

Alternate routes are advised.

Kristin Palm

Relativity

*"I love you," someone says, and instantly we begin
to wonder– "Well, how much?"—and when the answer
comes—"With my whole heart"—we then wonder
about the wholeness of a fickle heart*

—from In the Lake of the Woods
by Tim O'Brien

So the words are spoken,
with requisite hesitation,
tenacity: a sigh and then,
I think . . .
a pause, and then,
I know . . .

The earth does not move,
there are no fireworks,
not even sirens or drunks
yelling in the street.
Just wind gently pressing
against the panes, purple light,
stroking his hair
before fitful sleep,
and in the morning,
after coffee, one more kiss
at the door.

Kristin Palm

Lunar

His timing
couldn't have been better,
that crazy neighbor who leaves
tomatoes on our porch, shrieks
in German at kids in the street.
If I believed in God I'd swear
that's who sent him to the door
the morning you and I awoke
as strangers. He wanted to know
if I had seen the eclipse.
I'd been gauging the sky
all winter. He couldn't believe
I'd forgotten.

I didn't tell him
how we'd split the night with spitfire,
masking insecurities with accusations,
how I'd slept on the couch,
too shell-shocked to handle the heat
of your skin. That hardly mattered.
While our tiny world shifted on its axis,
the earth's dark veil slivered the heavens,
crimson shadow birthed the moon—luminous,
full, and infinitely larger

than you,

    or me,

or the swollen   space   between.

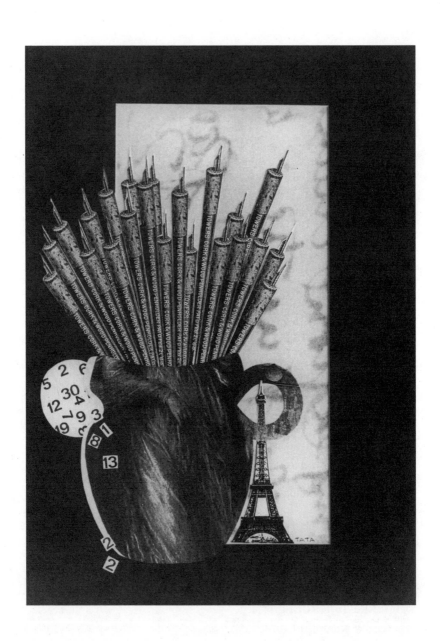

"Untitled," by Mary Tata, 1977.

Some Days Begin at my Toes

Photo © Wayne Field

Colleen Reader

Abstract Art

I understand how it happens:
You savor a sweet plum
picked fresh, noonday,
under keyholes of light
shagging through branches.
In the hush of night,
the worst news comes—
for the rest of your life
the ever-during dark
rings you awake.

Fruit with Still Life

Part of me is glad this is not another
"Still Life with Fruit and Wooden Bowl,"
"Still Life with Fruit and Linen Scarf,"
"Still Life with Fruit and Luminous Morning,"
always very dewy, with an apple
shadowed on one side and a miniature
white-paned window on the other—
the woman in this painting has good vibrations.

Kiwi, lime, mango are orbiting her head
on a cobalt blue background, or, could it be
dawn rising above her shoulders, with Mars
conspicuously red and wormholes leading
to universes outside our own? Balance,
composition, detail . . . still life
is not easy. Inside I am always vibrating,
each night better than the last.

Fringe

I've gone too far with fringe—
it dangles from bookshelves, lampshades,
portals, transoms, balustrades, frames
with family photos. Facing edgy things
with fringe delights my open hand
like creek-water splashing against it.
Each strand streams between fingers;
turn my palm downward, fringe spills over
knuckles, trickles up-arm, pools onto my face.
Twisted satin threads puddle between lips.
Some days begin at my toes, as though
I'm able to grasp still waters,
hold it as love is held. My husband calls
fringe a decorating obsession;
I believe in its potential.

Cocktail Hour

Just the facts. No need to embellish
the truth or sacrifice reality for riper tidbits
of hearsayeth and thou sayeth and whomever sayeth
in the name of the Lord—just give it to me neat.

Save your paper umbrella and sword of cherries
because a woman my age wants to know why
a man my age leaves for someone half our age.
It seems so with-it to rev-up the old hormones

and ride a Harley after the last graduation balloon
deflates. Besides thin and perky, what is the attraction?
Yesterday I overheard, *Mick Jagger—who is he?*
and left the butcher with fat-free kielbasa

contemplating liposuction on hips and belly—
worried about new fat cells settling in my hollow
cheeks and trim neck, now the best parts of this body.
The unpredictable has always made me crazy.

Down-to-earth is how my husband describes me.
Maybe that is so. Lately, I've been making friends
with gravity. Maybe in time I'll maneuver like a seagull
through fog slowly lifting, unburdened in the half-light.

Colleen Reader

Staying Up Past My Bedtime

There ought to be a law against
sinuous golden bodies with wavy hair
tied in ponytails streaked with gold . . . all that gold,
drinking beer and playing hackey-sac under yellow lights,
looking like secrets on the heels of night.
Especially in June, when hot pink peonies
are ready to burst, grass is embarrassingly soft
and steamin', and air smells of the first real night
of summer . . . because my tan lines have faded,
and traces of the '60's linger.

There ought to be a law against
big chromed engines with empty
squeeze seats . . . all that power and leather,
roaring in the night, throttling gears
after every stop sign, waking the dead.
Especially at 2 am, when I lie awake
from all the coffee I had at work,
now wondering about Utah,
and if it's true about gettin' kicks
on Route 66 . . . there ought to be a law against
what I'm thinking.

Modus Operandi

July morning, his windows open in a used sedan,
with one suitcase, a trumpet, too little money,
and hundreds of tapes securely filed within reach—
this is how a son leaves home for Sedona,
to open space, to earth and dust as red as light
from distant Mars. He promises to call.

Upstairs,
I am surprised to find his room in the same state
of affairs: laundry, pocket change, bath towels (so
this is where they go), and a creature I made
years ago scrunched (helplessly) between the wall
and unmade bed and the pillow he forgot.
Now I remind myself, as the crow flies, he is just
hours away from home. He promises to call.

Orion's Sword shines brighter in mountainous sky,
where he roams under constellations of his own.
Soon he'll climb redrocks, roast burritos on a stick,
and drag his flat belly through passages less wide
than his shoulders, as tribesmen did before him.

Easter,
the spring of the first Woodstock and man
walking on the moon, a gardenia flowered when I
first laid my son in his cradle. A tender celebration,
greenery foiled in blue, with *care instructions*
attached to the stem, promised new blossoms.

Nighttide

Colleen Reader

When I look at heaven,
stars shored up in darkness,
I want to call my father out
to the porch where I sit
and offer the night starring
as if it were his Thanksgiving
cigar and Drambuie.
Father all those years
gently working the glider,
back and forth into the nighttide
reflected under the moon's light
like a swan mirrored in water.
Now pressed against my own mirror,
I can't help reflecting myself.
Past my ear and over my shoulder
I see sunrises. Glorious pumpkin,
cranberry, buttery biscuit sunrises.
Just ahead the stark orange sun
sets balanced on the south train track
where the Chessie Cat travels asleep.
The rails silver. My marriage silvers.
Hair by hair I silver. After dinner
the sterling service is put away
into a cherry box lined with velvet.
Back and forth into the nighttide,
just like Dad. Heaven's light
fractures my sense, and I want to sip
Drambuie with my father.

Losing the Familiar

Bitten into like a midget dill, the skin parts
on my lip. I purse both lips to hide
the blood and wish for eyeglasses
that I denied for two years.
Just get us back to the old Hudson's store,
Mom says. *I know my way home*

from there. I'm lost driving home—
no phone, no map, lost in dark parts
on a Stephen King street. Abandoned stores
are sprayed with foul words; boarded fronts hide
the familiar past. *Do you remember the year*
Ben Hur won Best Picture? Her glasses

focus her eyes on memories. The car's glass is
clouding inside. I fear her memories of home
and chit-chat about grave blankets. Another year
gone, another block gone, the only familiar part
is getting Mom home. My tears are hidden
from her, like after Dad's funeral. Tears stored

away like too many jars of stewed tomatoes. *Stores*
had elevator ladies, she says, then lifts her glasses
and rubs her eyes. I bite my lip to hide
my horror towards her calm. *Nobody home,*
Dad teases as he knocks on my head; his ghost departs.
Glass is a liquid that behaves like a solid. Once a year

she sends blankets to the dead. Her years
settle in like the properties of glass. Abandoned stores
evoke a flush; I steer straight through the parts
about the grave blankets. The car's glass is
clearing inside. I find my way home.
This is how—I turn back. Detour signs hide

undercover like cash in her Crockpot. Breathy hums hide
between details of her Living Will and my New Year's
reconciliations with my myopia. *Home
is this way.* Sensing her eye's on the old Hudson's store,
I listen for directions. *Your sister needs glasses,*
she points her finger north, we leave behind the familiar parts

for home to where the living tell their stories
and the dead leave behind last wishes. Years once hidden
have become like glass. Ahead a narrow street parts.

Motor City Sky Line

Watchmaker's Wife

The watchmaker's wife wore a hairnet that webbed across her forehead and tangled into her eyebrows like patches of crooked oak grass gone wild under a chain-linked fence. Her tar-black pupils, round and transparent as a crystal face on a pocket watch, gave her the ability to hypnotize and save the souls of bored children—coaxing their attention with promises of prizes from her deep apron pockets in exchange for a lay of her hand on their sweaty heads. I believe that particular summer Helen saved more small souls on her back porch steps than Billy Graham after his Saturday broadcast. In truth, Helen was a curiosity to small souls. Her eyes and her apron pockets were beckoning and deep. I often confused the two.

Helen's presence was most evident on Easter Sunday (when it came late in April), Memorial Day, Independence Day, Labor Day, any summer weekend. In the hot and muggy days of August, she would pass time on her back porch step, watching white shirts and white sheets hang dry.

When the allure of softball, hula hoops, *Archie* comic books and pantomiming to Connie Francis came to be a bore and our fresh anticipation for new paper binders, long yellow pencils with soft unbitten erasers, and pointy crayons spread like a summer virus, we would help Helen watch the whites hang dry. On breezy days her memorized scripture, from the King James Version, whipped around our heads like laundry blowing bravely into the wind.

Once after a whisky-voiced, back-porch version of "Amazing Grace," she reached deep into her apron pocket and pulled out a tissue, dabbed the sweat from the back of her neck, dipped again into her apron pocket, then handed me the prize—a miniature set of plastic salt and pepper shakers. The prize for our attentions to the beheading of John the Baptist was a hand mirror encased in a plastic-coated picture of Jesus. The destruction of the temple was realized with a new kind of clothespin—red and when pinched, it opened. It was the '50's and plastics were the future.

Children never knew what Helen was going to pull from her apron pocket, and her green-card husband, the watchmaker, never knew what his wife was going to pull. One Saturday just before the noon siren—a signal to alert citizens of a Russian or Martian invasion—Helen called the city police in hopes of having my younger sister arrested for picking a yellow tulip from her garden.

At the end of summer, I knew the face of a clock without numbers confused Helen. She asked how its hands knew where to go and how yellow tulip bulbs knew which way to grow. In autumn she was taken from her home, right at the time when she buried yellow bulbs deep into pockets in her garden.

O

Tonight is a cool pillow against my cheek. I reach deep inside the pillowcase and pretend it's an apron pocket. Chimes and coos from fancy timepieces strike in the night and bruise the silence. The watchmaker pulls the door shade and moves the plastic hands to a time past on the pretend clock that reads: *I will return & Thank-you, Come Again.*

Adirondack chair

Adirondack Chair

Colleen Reader

Stay put in that Adirondack chair
after cottagers lock their shutters for winter,
and the floating dock leans against our cellar door,
after mosquitoes and campfires . . .
when altocumuli mound above blue spruce
and geese fly in silvery symmetry

after the tending season of hanging pots—
geranium, coreopsis, impatiens & everbearing
strawberries that will bear no more,
hibachi degreased and beach sand swept
between cracks on the steps . . . when climbing
roses stop climbing

after the first night-frost and vermilion sunrises—
the slow burn of vapory nights . . . when Mullet Lake
appears before you like a blank page in a day planner

after a crow's incessant caws arouse a dreamscape
to our favorite park bench, *sur l'île de la cité de Paris*,
along the Seine, where a Parisian dog in a beret
is barking its fool head off *en français* we kidded,
at French-green leaves gusting like laughter in cold air,

after a warped screen door echoes a morning chorus
and a caw shears the wind.

Colleen Reader

Jesus Upon His Retirement

He looks forward to the end of this place;
he dreams of the handshake, initialed watch
and cake sliced at two o'clock. The offering
for thirty years is summed in a retiree's
spreadsheet and detailed for beneficiaries—
themselves returned home with MA's,
and failed marriages. He contemplates
how nice life will be to roll over in bed,

cover his head just as the winter sun cuts
through his eyelids.
He is anxious to use his hands:
play piano, sketch, plant a garden,
refinish furniture and navigate by the stars
like DeGama, charting the ocean's scars
at the round of the Cape of Good Hope.
He imagines himself with a glass of Merlot

in one hand, a Walkman attached to his belt,
whistling the song of every state's bird, and keen
in the politics of Arabic and African countries.
He is ready to pump iron at a well-juiced health spa,
quit cigarettes, and lower his cholesterol by eating
no dairy and by power-walking at the mall.
Soon. Very soon. He'll have a senior's discount
card that he'll proudly pull out at Bill Knapp's.

His endless addition of points has gone
beyond the pale, reminiscent of the scene
in *Ben Hur,* on the Roman slave ship,
when the drums were striking a beat
with oars cutting deep into the Adriatic—

one point for a year's labor plus
one point for staying alive,
sum must equal 85 for
full pension with medical.

Oh God, he sighs, through the chewed rim
on a foam cup, entranced with thoughts
of long-cooked oats, wolfhound at his heel,
looking forward to the remainder of his life.

Hands

I

When I pray the Lord's Prayer,
> *Our Father who art in heaven*
my hands seem mismatched
> *Hallowed be thy name*
not as one navy and one brown sock
> *Thy kingdom come*
or a new towel hangs
> *Thy will be done*
beside an old towel,
> *On earth as it is in heaven*
but more like a recognized voice
> *Give us this day our daily bread*
speaking from an unfamiliar face,
> *And forgive us our debts*
or like children's cut-outs
> *As we forgive our debtors*
with animal parts pasted to people,
> *And lead us not into temptation*
to see my hands as women's hands
> *But deliver us from evil*
that unearth the war's harvest
> *For thine is the kingdom*
for missing sons and polish the marking stones
> *And the power*
on neighbors' graves is to see a hedgerowed field
> *And the glory*
and the quarry on which it grows.
> *For ever and ever Amen*

II

Yet, beneath this manicure
my hands mirror my mother's:
the crested moons,
the spared paths,
the splay of our fingers palm to palm, gene to gene,
the half-curled pinkie when stirring coffee.

Full Circle

Colleen Reader

Day 1

The fire pit blazes with familiar sounds,
the family is reminiscing—even the little ones
have stories to tell. In the cabin I sit
at a chrome-legged table with desires
to write the tradition I see, my Monet.
The middle children are playing flashlight tag,
their shadows long and lean as Argentina . . .
the grown children are comforting their exhausted babies.

Tonight a full moon floats on the rim of the earth,
black water is veiled in silver. I watch a silhouette
move parallel to the horizon; its sails have hidden the moon.
The first night is a new lover wooing the possibilities.
My words, I think, diminish the meaning.

Day 2

The early birds slip from their nests
for quiet, tea and secrets under the umbrella.
Shortbread is sliced into pie wedges
before men and children wake.

The gulls line the breakwater like double-
yolked eggs in an old-fashioned gray carton.
Real cream for the coffee and bacon sizzles.
The children beg Popsicles for breakfast

and the birds justify it all just because.
The sunrise promises a scorcher.
Lake Huron shimmers like a million sapphires.

Day 3

The sun rises across Lake Huron—aqueous slate
subtle as felt. Aimless as driftwood afloat, I count
the bobbing chests of sea gulls. Half-again are banking the breeze—
a baker's dozen on the breakwater. I have never determined

the event that bewitches more. Sunrise. Sunset.
The phases of the moon. The dynamics of presence,
the unknown generations, I speculate with melancholy.
Age has scripted Jessie to self-appoint as wood-gatherer

and fire-builder. My grown son, the oldest cousin,
self-appointed guardian of Grandpa's stories. Sometimes
life settles into a province no larger than a violet petal.
Nicole has brought me a strawberry dipped in chocolate.

Day 4

The day is wet. The windows are closed
against driving rain, the cabin doors left
ajar for the weary; cabin fever for some.
On the hem of the sky is a tugboat; I imagine
men in yellow slickers. Myself, I enjoy the change
in scenery.

Day 5

Independence Day. The Fourth of July. Mary
wears her flag earrings in the shape of hearts.
She has a thing about hearts. Every year
she busies herself hunting for stones shaped

as hearts to give to her grandchildren
for their pockets. One year she discovered
a Petosky stone—a curious find for this shore—
a stone indigenous to Lake Michigan . . .
I love her love for hearts.

Day 6

Here I sit at a chrome-legged table trying to find a suitable end
for this story. NPR comes to mind, details without resolution . . .
or as the first day back to school, *What I Did On Summer Vacation*.

This last night ends as the first night began . . . . Before sleep
I'll curl as a snail inside my jacket, close to the last glints
of the fire. Listen to the lake whisper the same *wish . . . wish . . .
wish . . .*
Watch the moon rise, coming full circle.

Colleen Reader

Stereoscope

There are times I'd prefer a night wild
to a night in the wilderness with my computer.
Already I'm chilled and a skeleton with roses
for hair is stalking the screen. An eager wind

rattles the window where my posture reflects
crumpled and raw edged,
as if to say, *Who are you kidding, I'm out of here.*
Still, my flesh and bone stay,

for some nights a new poem unfolds in the direction
of its own creases, like bellows on a camera
expanded to open a view or a pleated road map
where inside the journey ends at a circle.

But most nights a new poem is a map folded
in the wrong direction, a mountain crushed
into a valley, *Moonrise Over New Mexico*
without the regal moon, its light draping

over the pueblos of basket makers and sheep farmers,
the world without *Half Dome Glacier*
where Ansel took God's picture. To envision
the firing flash of light
and clouds of acrid smoke,
silvery emulsions,
water baths,
an infrared sphere burning
in darkened chambers

is like sliding a stereoscope into focus;
an inner voice offers dimension beyond
the edge of thin paper, to where there are new beginnings,
each one the surface of a mineral freshly broken.

Delicacy

photo © Wayne Field

Susan Paurazas

Uncharted Waters

Water churns and throws ideas against a coral reef, cuts their scarred surfaces. Salt stings in bloodless wounds with each poor choice, false turn, misdirection. Then the rocks are polished, worked over by repeated washing. The sea turns them over in its mouth, sucks meaning out of each rough phrase, tastes the sounds of uneven rhythm, savors the flavors of seaweed and sand over and over, until slate and granite roll off its tongue in layered slabs. Verbs are smooth and round as quartz beads. Jagged edges of broken speech are transformed to fit neatly in the corner of the cheek. Nouns slide down its gaping throat. Adverbs spew out in a fine pebble stream, modify the spring and leap of skipping stones. With each bounce, a whirlpool of meaning forms, intersects the churning surface. Ideas cross at edges in sudden waves, boomerang hidden treasure.

Being Herd

I told her I didn't know where her crystal elephant was, the hand-blown creation that once sat on an antique table in Grandma's living room. Delicate and fragile with an upturned trunk, Pinky was one of my favorites, made of lightly tinted rose glass. She could turn the sun into a rainbow of colors. That's what Pinky was doing as I held her to the window, turned her gently in my hands. It was then I heard the click of heels down the hall and scrambled to replace Pinky to her perch atop a lace doily, but my fingers brushed against the slippery lace. It slid on the polished wood, edges of lace curled and ruffled, taking Pinky aloft on a slow motion ride, Pinky streaming blue, yellow, orange, and violet in the afternoon sun on a fine, white magic carpet. It was silent and magical, her trunk upturned, her ears trailing in breezy air. In her final descent, I'm sure I saw her smile.

"Where is Pinky?" Grandma asked.

My trance was broken by her crisp words, like the rose splinters scattered over the floor. She didn't believe me when I told her about Pinky's magic carpet ride, how she had flown high, almost touched the sun, then had come back to earth like a falling star. But that's what had happened. Pinky had gotten her wish of traveling far from Grandma's living room, no longer confined to surroundings of dusty books, cuckoo clocks, drawn drapes, and needlepoint pillows. Pinky had returned on a white Persian rug to melting sun and sand, baskets and robes, marketplace chatter and caravans. I knew she was happy in those fleeting moments, living an ancient elephant life.

"Pinky," ink, watercolor by Susan Paurazas, 1996

Susan Paurazas

Laundry Day

"Go hang these up to dry," my mother says and hands me the brown wicker basket filled with freshly washed sheets, wet and sweet. The sheets are heavy as I carry the basket, stretching my skinny arms; the spikes of wicker jab my knees with each step. I look to my sister and nod toward the door. She knows what I mean and follows me into the yard, shuffles along, bounces a stray ball, throws a rock into the bushes, picks a dandelion. I keep walking.

"Come on," I say. She runs to me and holds the dandelion under my chin.

"You like butter," she says.

I smile and hand her a corner of the wet sheet. We stand between the two huge maple trees, look up, up where the clothesline is stretched taut, like a guitar string. Each with our end we turn and push, hurl the wet bunch over the top. The spray of water droplets stings our faces as the sheet snaps over the rope. Then with our hands we straighten and smooth the wrinkles, working together. We know the routine.

"It has to be even on both sides," I remind.

My sister absentmindedly tugs on her corner. We place the clothespins on each end, and one in the middle. The wood mouths pinch the fabric like hungry crickets. We snap at each other with the wooden bugs, chase in and out between the flapping sheets, in between and around until dizzy, we fall on our backs in the grass, giggling. Breathing fast and gulping air, we look up and watch the billowing white sheets move across the sky with the clouds.

Susan Paurazas

Sestina: Summer

There was nothing to do. Mother didn't give
me a chance to whine. *Ride your bike, run*
through the sprinkler, jump rope, or play
in the sandbox, she said. *Enjoy the summer*
now. Make hay while the sun shines. It won't last forever,
in three months you'll start school.

It seems like yesterday I was in school
waiting for summer vacation, trying to give
attention to the last math test, when forever
was on the other side of the window. I ran
out the front door when the last bell rang. Summer
had finally started, three whole months of freedom to play

with friends, dress up in old clothes and put on a play
for our parents in the garage. Thoughts of school
out of our minds, we savored every taste and smell of summer,
heard the jingle of the ice cream truck, begged Mom to give
us a dollar for a Bomb Pop or Eskimo Pie, ran
after the truck, smacked our lips on the iced delight. Forever

was something we didn't think of. Forever
was an hour until dinner, or anytime we played
Barbies, hopscotch, jacks or tag, ran
in between twirling double Dutch ropes. School
was just a distant possibility. We didn't give
it a second thought. It was summertime

and the living was easy. I was going to summer
Girl Scout camp for two whole weeks. Forever
friends in sleeping bags and log cabins gave
us the creeps telling ghost stories at night, plays
on words, riddles. We learned things you don't in school,
how to start a fire with sticks, toast marshmallows runny

and gooey, ride a horse, trot, gallop, and run,
move with it, the control in my hands, summer
streaking through my hair. I couldn't wait to tell at school
what I did in the summer that lasted forever,
how we sang songs in a circle while the troop leader played
the guitar, how we harmonized with marshmallow tongues. Gave

hugs to new friends, returned to school. I was forever
changed, ran forward, grew up, summer
as a golden place and time, dreams and chances given.

"Susan's Youth," silk screen print, Susan Paurazas,1978.

Susan Paurazas

The Kiss

It begins as a small thing,
a tiny crevice in a sideways glance
where only a sigh can filter through
particles that hang in a stream
of sunlight, vibrating between them.

It begins with the tilt of her head,
the angle of her neck, smooth
and graceful like a heron
paused before flight, as warm
breaths rise in winged vapors.

It begins with a closeness
as he bends near, the brush
of his hair against her cheek,
the nuzzle of noses as scents
drift sweet and tangy,
linger like distant memories
that gel in a liquid moment.

It begins with the caress of her hand
against his face, a wisp of hair as it falls
and frames the curve of her mouth,
a whisper so secret it triggers a thousand
sensations at once; as their lips
barely meet with a silken touch
their promise begins.

Susan Paurazas

Delicacy

In your hand, I am a peach
that you have selected,
soft and round, full
and ripe, flushed with oranges
and reds. The promise
of my sweetness
fills your head, pools
in your mouth. You turn me
over in your hand, survey
my perfection, stroke my skin.
You feel the soft, fuzzy curves,
and I can see the pleasure
in your eyes, the expectation,
the wanting of that first
lovely bite. Your mouth opens
to savor me. Sweet juice
drips down your chin. Eyes
closed, you cannot hear
the peeling away
of my soul.

Susan Paurazas

Secret Recipe

I make sweet bread,
a favorite recipe
that we once enjoyed together
on Sunday with herbal tea.

I start with fine, sifted flour
mixed with courser grains.
I add warmed milk to yeast,
not too hot, or it will die—
sensitive, like me,
cannot take extremes.

I massage and knead
the sticky dough, feel it spring
back in my hands, expand
and squeeze between my fingers,
pour a cup of sugar for days
of sweetness. Tears salt
the mix—sorrow, loss,
the way we both let go.

I chop walnuts, add zest
of lemon, surprise the senses
with tangy humor. Then fold
in favorites, raisins and dates
for dots of color, fiber, texture.

The dough rises and swells, doubles
its size, flows over the rim—
the way we grew together, doubled
ourselves into one. I divide and tear
the dough into halves, roll out each piece
then twist the lengths around themselves
in a continuous spiral braid.

As I work, I expect you to surprise
me with a warm embrace, feel the
velvet of your touch. It's just a dream;
instead I shine the top with egg,
bake my luscious creation.
I cut into the steamy bread, slice
a piece for each of us.

Plate set before your empty chair,
I read aloud to you and sip chamomile tea.
I savor the fragrance with each bite,
chew the warm, honeyed treat.
Butter melts and coats my mouth,
drips a sweet familiar caress.
I taste your kiss again.

Susan Paurazas

The Scent of Granny's Roses

I arrange red roses in a vase,
finger soft petals, inhale
their sweet smell. The house
is dark and still except
for the tick-tock of an iron pan
with numbers and hands that
hypnotize with a steady rhythmic beat.

The night shimmers from
the flush of a plum full moon;
I stand still as the pine
outside my window, become
part of the luminous glow,
fade into hidden shadow as
a cloud passes over the moon.
I think of my grandmother,
asleep at Garden City Hospital.

The touch of a midnight breeze
cools my skin. The scent of roses fills the room;
I turn until I see the clock stopped on one.
The tick is gone, the window's closed,
yet wind whispers over my skin.
The fleeting shiver of Grandmother's soul
touches mine. My breath is slow
as I inhale her rose perfume.

I know she's here; I try to speak
through the thickness of my tongue.
No words can form; I only
hear my pounding pulse, the spell
of her passing on. I try to touch her
one last time, but she is gone,
and I am left standing
in the ice blue night.

Elizabeth Paurazas, July 22, 1922

Susan Paurazas

Month of Sundays

She sits in her chair by the window,
as the rain taps an offbeat rhythm,
and she searches out through the misty fog
for a sign of a dark blue sedan.
It must, she thinks, be an April rain
preparing May flowers for spring,
grape hyacinths and daffodils.
She'll wear her purple dress today
when he comes to take her to church.

Women used to wear hats to church
and embroidered white lace gloves.
Aunt Lucille showed her how
to spin fine creations with the lace
and shared her prize-winning recipe
for honey-glazed currant rolls.

It seems like she smells them now,
then looks up to see the friendly nurse
with a breakfast tray enter her room,
chirping, *How are we today, dear?*
Obediently she swallows pale green pills
crushed in a bowl of applesauce,
then eats scrambled eggs and a slice of dry toast,
pretends it's a fresh currant roll.

In the TV room, she has a preoccupied
chat with Mary and Norm. Thinks she hears
a motor hum. Now and then glances out
windows in search of her son.
When the evening news comes on, she knows
it's time to return to her room.

She smoothes her napkin over her lap
to prevent spoiling her purple dress.
Then slowly eats her meal. Peers out
at the empty parking lot for shines
of approaching headlights. Puzzled,
she thinks, it must not be Sunday.
He never came to take her to Mass.

She unfolds the lacy, yellowed square,
lays her rosary on the tray and gently
strokes the crystal beads, thinks
of tulips and daffodils. She dabs
her eyes with tender lace, says a prayer
for Aunt Lucille, and hopes
tomorrow is Sunday.

Angels in the Snow

Susan Paurazas

Today in the pocket of my winter coat
I find white feathers nestled
between mittens and soft silk lining,
a delicate sanctuary that waits
for a blue teardrop, a robin's egg.

Woven pine branches
of a Christmas wreath
hang on my door, waiting
for snowflakes to end
and feathers to begin as
chickadees pluck at their berries.

Icicle spears drip angel tears
on crocus cups, trickle
a promise of spring forgiveness
with slow, clear drops of knowing.

I walk in a path illuminated
by unseen light. A sudden breeze
swirls between the snap
of a twig and my skin—
to settle in deep,
like forgotten songs.

My boots sink in the white
melt of snow, cushion
like layered wings
of lilt and down. Memories
of angels made in the fluffy
white of childhood

lead me to believe in heaven,
my own angelic guardians.
They bring the heat of a closer
sun, by brilliant revelation.

Perennial

Susan Paurazas

Each year in the spring
crocuses bloom, songbirds
return, signal new life
and new beginnings.
Except for one spot
by the side of the road.

Each year greenery appears;
two wreaths are placed
on the edge to remember
who died there one
morning in May.

I remember the day. I
avoided that route. A serious
accident was all they said
on the radio. Later I heard
two people died in the crash
that morning on the entrance ramp.

I wonder if anyone else
sees the interwoven green
near the *merge right* sign,
feels the power she steers
with her hands, how easily
a twig can snap, a blossom
wilt, a robin's egg crack.

As the traffic flies and buzzes along,
I tell myself one day I'll drive by
slowly on a Sunday morning,
when orange rays split the darkness,
when I can creep close and see
who they are, reflect on the families
whose memories live, and softly
whisper, *I'm sorry.*

Susan Paurazas

Quiet Midnight

I hold you in quiet
midnight and hum
lullabies that drift
to soft, hidden ears,
hush tiny cries.

You know my secrets,
have lived among
their hidden spirits.
Your eyes speak to me
of the lost ones,

babies I never had, ones
who didn't have a chance.
They slipped away
into tiny crevices,
claimed their own
small territory. They
never leave. I will them
to stay and can't forget
the spark of their stirring.

Susan Paurazas

Reunion

for Allison

The cream of my skin flows
into yours, warm flushes
of your butterfly breaths flutter
across my chest. Your hand
touches the spot under my ribs
where you used to kick
and reminds me of when
we were always together
linked by more than a pulsing cord.

Belly to belly, our heartbeats thump
in rhythm to hungry tugs
and with each one, I want to
take you back into myself,
bring you again into my flesh
undivided and complete.

But with each rise and fall
and sweet exhale, each caress
of hand to head and mouth
to breast, I know it is enough
to be this way, and I am
swallowed back into wholeness
in the sigh of a smile.

Susan Paurazas

Purple Haze

There isn't much to leave:
a small dental office with a private line,
a view box, journals, a comfortable chair.
No family photos or memorable quotes
to *tie a knot and hang in there,*
just a picture of Hendrix taped to the wall
behind the door by a cohort friend,
a reminder of the craziness that comes when

I tap dance between endless
faces, explain treatment options,
Medicaid guidelines, financial arrangements,
move sleekly through the magenta maze.
Perfectly timed, I know when to catch,
when to leap, when to bow, with a phrase
or a nod, *He's here again, might be a problem,*
I'll take this one, I've seen her before.

Step lightly to the maniac waltz
between lime green chiffon and the bag man
in long johns who carries his life in a bucket.
A woman who claims she can't beat the pain
without narcotics (she'll tell you which ones).
The single mom with three small kids

desperate for help. I proceed to the one
with the swollen face, a broken jaw,
she won't tell me how, until I suggest
she might have been hit and wasn't
just clumsy. She denies it at first,
then leans to my ear and whispers, *yes,*
once we're alone and truth burns through.

I've got this down to a work of art
a free-form dance to handle this
and soothe that. Exhausted from
the intricate steps, I slip into
the soft blue chair to
document the day's events,
charts piled high
on top of my desk.

My last step done, I take a bow
to phantom cheers, silent applause.
No encore for my final performance,
Jimi stares. I close the door
and walk away, exit this purple
haze.

A Lot of Little Things

Susan Paurazas

Charlie's Crab is buzzing with the lunch time crowd. It's busy for a Tuesday. I sit in the booth and drink a glass of ice water with a twist of lemon. I gently hold the glass to my face to cool myself. My throat is parched and tight. It's summer, and I'm hot and drained. I look over at you as you survey the menu. I've been here with you at our favorite restaurant so many times. Today nothing appeals to us. Should we stay or go somewhere else? We decide to stay. It's too much work to find another place, and I'm tired. I don't have the energy to hunt. I decide to have the soup and sandwich special, crab meat melt on an English muffin. You have the same. I can't remember which chowder is red, which is white. It's strange that I don't know this now. Nothing looks interesting.

Our hands meet in the center of the table. We talk about a lot of little things. I cannot bring myself to talk about the test results. Neither can you. Lunch arrives. It doesn't taste as good as I remember. Still, it fills me up. I remind you that we'd better go or we'll be late for the appointment. We walk out onto the street. I clutch my purse with one hand, hold your hand with the other. We walk into the scorching heat. My mouth is dry again; I cannot speak.

Susan Paurazas

Leaving Chance

I won't go back there this time. I won't
get drawn back into the dark corners,
the cold, clammy walls I clung to, the dark
recesses I loved to hide in, waiting
in doubt, sure of nothing.

Moss webbed my fingers, the musty
scent of denial filled my lungs.
It was my refuge. Sometimes
I miss the lonely drops
of water, the scurry of chance
across the hard, dirt floor.

It calls to me every winter when
the wind moans through secret hollows.
When I crawled out for the last time,
I knew I wouldn't go back to feel
the chill of its walls. I'd thrown away
the map.

"Dreamscape," Watercolor, by Susan Paurazas, 1996.

Susan Paurazas

Each Small Choice

I wonder how I got to this place in my life,
this town, this job, this home, but it is no mystery.
There was no secret passage, no hidden stairway,
no alien abduction that landed me here. It happened
slowly, methodically, with each small choice,
each slight turn with a blink or a shrug or a nod,
almost imperceptible to the naked eye. Tiny,
insignificant clues that tie the mystery together,
link the intricacy of my life, the novel of my being.

Sometimes I want to read the book backwards
from the last page, so I can tell myself when not
to open the closet, skip whole chapters, edit
and rewrite with a thick, red pencil, show where X
marks the spot—and why X is important. Stick
arrows in the forks in the road, so I can tell myself what I'm
looking for, and why I'm reading this endless manuscript.

But then I realize that truth is better than fiction.
It sticks to my ribs, burns in my heart, and melts
in my mouth. It exposes the fluff and fantasy
of a dime store novel and lays plain
courage and character like buried treasure,
unearthed artifacts. And so I write the next word,
turn the next page, and create
myself with a purposeful stroke.

Standing on the Edge

Susan Paurazas

Standing on the edge
of the event horizon,
I peer into a great, black hole.
If I take a step forward,
tomorrow will suck me into
its gaping, hungry darkness,
consume me in one gulp.

But I can't step back
or turn and run. Today
pulls me toward the whirling
center of its hidden secrets
and agendas. I've come too far.
I want to go back, but I know
I can't. The past collapses inward
to infinite density. Then in a brash moment
the edge is gone and I am naked singularity,
a glimpse of quantum truth.

Exposed, I submit to the big bang
momentum. I lift my foot and point
a toe to test the space where time and light
are captive, feel nothing below,
and with arms spread wide, leap.

"Untitled" pen and ink drawing, by Kim Kurczyski, 1997.

A Guide to the Modern Life

photo © Kim Kurczyski

Denise Thomas

Illuminations for the Practicing Poet

Page number 33 tells me how I can recover fugitive memories. I want to know—where have they been all these years? What towns and cities have they fled to, how many have they seen? Under what assumed names have they avoided capture? What sort of work have they found to support themselves? Is there no statute of limitations for fugitive memories, no consideration of circumstance, no credit given for a quiet, non-criminal life since they went on the lam? The recovery of fugitive memories may not serve justice as well as one may think; anything that lives a furtive life for so long may no longer be the thing it once was. How will I know my fugitives from anyone else's? How many are out there, going about their business day by day, going to work, cleaning house? How many are out there, hidden in shacks, living under bridges, in basements, the crotches of dead trees?

A Guide to the Modern Life

Denise Thomas

Ironing clothes is High Magick. Spirits called by the warm smell
of clean, smooth fabric will grant any desire.

If Joy gets in your eyes, rinse thoroughly. Do not exceed
the recommended dosage.

Starve the snails for at least eight days. To prevent shock hazard,
do not expose to rain or moisture.

If you wish to hang up this picture, make a hole here ●
When asked, enter the appropriate four-digit code.

Two peas in a whale pod make a strong soup.
It's best to add a cup of fresh water and three large carrots.

Night Blindness

My mother used a saucepan to put out the fire in the backyard. We
were more careful next time, and set the blaze in the neighbor's yard.

The neighbors had a tree that towered over both our houses.
All summer it hummed like a green dynamo.

I panhandled through high school with the story I needed bus fare.
I never took that bus, but I took that money over and over and over.

I'd considered climbing out the window but opted for the front door
instead. The ditches I hid in were green awash in moonlight.

I put my feet as far forward in the car as I can.
With night-blindness I have to feel my way along the road.

If I could write the paintings of Remedios Varo, I could remember
the revolutions we dreamed so long ago on air-filled nights.

Denise Thomas

Requiem

Did you hear about the Loch Ness Monster?
The announcement of her death
struck my heart
and left smears as black as the tabloid ink.
How can such an essential creature die?
She never claimed to be anything she wasn't—
unlike that *Abominable Snowman*, who isn't
made of snow.
She made her occasional appearance for the cameras,
bumped the odd boat or two,
played hide-n-seek with the sonar
in a shy fetus sort of way.
Eluded all her suitors.
The rest of her family, still in the Loch,
declined interviews and photos—
they always do.
But there was poor Nessie,
splashed across the front page,
lifeless on the beach.

In despair I held a seance,
me and a few friends, aficionados
of Kraken and sea serpents.
Now I see visions of Nessie in my oolong;
she dances on the ice cubes in my juice.
I see her surface in the neighbor's
bird bath.
She lolls in my bathtub and crowds me;
preferring long, languorous soaks,
she is not fond of showers.

I wanted her around, but I didn't
want her to take over my life—

there must be room for things
in addition to leviathans and minotaurs,
mermaids and the monsters of Loch Ness.
Womon does not live on visions alone.
I must come out of the forest
and pay the electric bill.
I must climb down
from Nessie's broad back and sweep
the front porch of ancient leaves.
Occasionally I must end my conversation
with the bees
and pour their honey on toast.

Denise Thomas

(Gazing through Veils)

Rising from the pavement, the floorboards, Homer's
wine dark seas,
my dead bounce through fog banks, ride
wavering breezes clothed in yellow leaves
and housedresses, make grand entrances
into my dreams.
My dead sit down to coffee with me, tuck
me into makeshift beds, ride my shoulders
like Housework Harpies.

Drifting dust has clouded my memory.
Is it the dust raised by your running,
by your dance that kept you
just out of reach; or by her worn broom; or
by that other's whirling headdress of disapproval?
All this dust fogs the mirror of memory.

Eleanor, she of the worn broom, in uniform of housedress and apron and sagging bosom, veiled in life by
my mother and that sheer steel mesh shimmering
in the middle of Main Street. A veil woven of *Mama
knows best*, and *You're my little boy*, stretched
on the loom of wrong-side-of-the-tracks.
As wispy in Death as she was to me in life.

Hazel, the Housework Harpy, a uniform of slacks
for the money job, housedress for the home and that
whirling headdress.
Veils gauze-like but strong; veils of compulsion, obsession,
fear, disapproval. The Weft is Bigotry, the Warp is
what will people think? woven on a loom
of sweat and disinfectant. I exorcise her
with Salvation Army furniture and cat tracks
in the house dust.

Theresa, veiled by the dust of her running and the dust
that veils the mirror of the past, the veils she trailed
about herself as she lived. Her veils woven
of surgical steel,
and darting eyes strung on rods of guilt,
her loom a mantra of *I'm shit, I'm bad, I deserve*
no better than this.
I reach for her and my fingertips
strike the mirror hidden by veils. I rip them away;
she retreats like water sucked into a drain.
The mirror is blank. My face casts no reflection here,
not now.

I am heavy with the dead.
Three is all I can eat at one sitting.
My other dead mill about the edges of the world.
Do they think they are not welcome?
Coming in threes through the veil that thins at
the turn of the wheel,
they visit the others who own them this dead year.

Denise Thomas

Sense Assault (Urban)

I spend my time looking out windows,
sniffing through my screens,
listening to the cars and car stereos blast
up and down the street . . .
I burn incense to override the fragrance
of auto exhaust and grease-fried foods,
the odor of dog feces floating over the fences.
I study silence to build a wall
and so I sometimes can think in even broad daylight.

I ride my back porch occasionally;
the bare wood transmits the earth to the starving roots
in the bottom of my feet.
The trash in the front yard
multiplies no matter how often I harvest it;
my feet ache for that struggling grass.

The faithful trees that shield the house
from cold winds and fierce
solar bombardments
are slowly dying—
but I can't bring myself to cut them down.
I watch them leaf out less and less
each year; they weave a green curtain
I can inhale.

My postage stamp of earth
couldn't sustain a trumpet vine
angry at being sliced back
and dragged from under the house-siding.
The comfrey lost the battle with a man—
as will my lilac tree
that blooms with birds and birdsong
beneath my bedroom.

The stars feel overwhelmed
and barely show themselves.
Lucky for me, the moon
doesn't fear cities.

Sleeping in August

I turn the pillow around.
I turn me around.
I need air
and fog-gowned treetops,
even if they are
illumined by false moonlight,
false sunrise,
security lights of insecure neighbors.
I press my Tarot pack between my knees
as air moves across my face,
as fog pads into
the room.
Waiting for the tiny chill
of August-close morning.

Denise Thomas

Titus Andronicus redux

You expect me to talk
about this? I'll rip your throat
out. I'll rip my throat out. No,
no danger of that. The words
can't get out anyway. I'm too
angry to wade through the morass
again. I'm too battered to swim.

What is it you want to know?
I'm alive. There's a full moon
and I'm sober; I don't have
the intoxication
of exhilarated, youthful trust
tainting my bloodstream.

Call me Lavinia,
although I escaped
with my hands. You can't see
my mutilations. My tongue
wags free until I wrap it around
certain words, combinations of
syllabi, letters in a peculiar order.

My father would bake those dainties
of villain's flesh; but such
ingredients could suck no revenge,
nor poison a villainous mother.

My RAGE
could destroy the world;
my fear festers
into storms frenzied with my own blood.
I stab myself with pens.
I escaped with my hands,

but they snap every pencil.
My fingers can tap out
no messages on tabletops;
my spirit won't respond
except with splintered teeth
and death threats from beyond.

Bioadhesive Carnal Pharmaceutica

Denise Thomas

Compare firsts.

The *first time* she opens.

The first time *she opens*.

Opening should be the beginning of her quest.

The *first* opening fails to give any clue to the whereabouts of that elusive object, that new world brave and stellar.

Opening proves the easy way to be blinded, proves a great illusion dazzling the mind.

This opening requires an abandonment, a slipping away to which she never consents.

It may bring knowledge, but it is bitter.

Sex is an acquired taste, like cigars, whiskey, opera.

Unlike sex, whiskey, opera, it takes no trying to get the taste for the needle.

the taste for the needle	*slowly drawn up in stainless*
sting of stainless, tiny bite of	*steel, a thorn,*
long-legged spider spinning	*up to sweet sweet nectar*
into a future, the past	*gathered long ago, dripping fine and clear*
swept up and cocooned like a morsel	*pheromones waft on the air, hunting,*
to be sucked later, the future a morsel	*drawing those with the proper receptors*
not yet wound, dangling on the edge	*the taste for the sting*

The illusion is more compelling, the promises so blatantly transparent the edge feels less lethal, a dull blade sawing the future.

She opens smoothly, only the veins play coy.

The knowledge stays sweet a long time.

The knowledge smooths rough blood.

She opens, she is permeable, she is soft stone.

She sighs as she is sculpted.

Cartography

Denise Thomas

I Maps

They say
entire galaxies are lost down the gullets of black holes.
But whoever really loses a galaxy?
Car keys, hair, teeth, the other sock,
the dog,
the love of your life, your common sense.
These are the things that go lost,
that move from here to nowhere
on the maps I carry.
I don't have a map of Lost.
Every time it's a new journey
and I'm just waving good-bye.

II Map Symbols

Find an invisible thing.
Put your finger on it and sniff it carefully.
Consider how the odor shifts
from lustful hate to a sterility
like that which flutters from the dry braincases of dead men.
It will begin to wiggle,
so grasp it firmly
until it calms,
and the shape flows over your hands
and begins to smell of green
and sweet
and salt
and slips through your astonished fingers
to coil about your feet,
an invisible source of revelation,
yours forever

until you flutter from your body,
and it is once again an invisible thing
waiting to be found.

III Artifacts

Pieces of green jade
should be held
and fondled.

Alone and uncaressed
they moan
and shatter.

Pieces of blue jade
should be carried
in pairs.

Single stones alone
are weepy
and bleak.

Pieces of red jade
should be hidden
in clothing.

Without the human touch
they wither
and weaken.

Pieces of green jade should be held
to the heart,

gently carved in the likeness
of one's favorite season,

warmed in the hands of vengeful
deities,

offered fresh blossoms,

laid to rest under willows.

It's Just a Phase . . .

Bathing in pools of Moonvolts,
i watch the moony mist
seep into the palms of my hands.
It stains the soles of my feet
like silvered henna tattoos.
Splashes spill over
and tint the pool rims.
The vapor creeps up the bones of my arms.
The veins in my thighs throb.
My lungs glow inside my amethyst ribs
and my eyes loose clouds
that drape the stars flowing from my mouth.

Rising from my bath, i go Moonriding.
Tap-dancing on Her shrinking belly,
i'm a little spacey.
It's just a lack of gravity,
and maybe too much darkmoon wine.
Stuffed full of harvest grain
and black bread, i rest my feet
on the Moon's horns
until She grows so thin i slide back to earth.

Nodding Beauty

Denise Thomas

> *Heroin smacks of glamour, both the ancient glamour*
> *of a spell of enchantment, and the modern glamour*
> *of romance and excitement*

Most stories begin *Once upon a time*.
This one begins with a yawn.

She pricked her finger
On the Singer and fell asleep for thirty years.
Spiny urchins marched themselves
Around the castle. Spiny urchins became
That barrier of thorns so often talked about in later years.
All her mail went unanswered.
Books flapped the corridors unread.
Her father moved the household
Into a distant monastery
And spent his time organizing expeditions
Into interior closets.
Her mother spent a few days dialing
Her after breakfast,
Letting the phone ring—and ring—and ring
Until the dust clouds obscured the ceilings.
Beauty believed it was a ringing in the cook's ears.
Her sister was convinced that Beauty was a changeling child.

Howling princes circled
The castle perimeters.
Her subjects stood with heads bowed
And took her rambling commands
To heart.
Dragging pumpkins behind them,
They stabled rats in their larders.

The treasury was emptied.
She handed brick after brick of gold to that Wizard Spoonful—

That bloodless poppy she had kissed and turned
Into the Wizard of the Disposable Wand
And itchy nose.
Mercenaries did her somnambulistic bidding,
Steadfastly following the script of her murderous dreams.

The dungeons glowed.
By ones, by threes, by legions and mobs,
Ministers and knights, Minstrels and ladies–in–waiting,
Court portrait painters and Scribes, washerwimmin and
Wisewimmin,
Nurses and nannies,
All fed the Executioner's fires.
Knights of the Glass Lance
Held jousts for her amusement,
Fell off their feet, their horses long ago eaten.
(The only horse left in her realm was that which
Rode her like a loa rides the possessed.)
The squires worked the crowds
As pickpockets.

She went to the Ball with the Hungry Tiger.
At dawn her gown turned to rags.
The glitter of chandeliers was merely
The sparkle of broken needles.
She rode the Tiger back
To the Wizard and bad magick,
Dropping her syringe behind her.

The glass shattered and played
A jarring music
That disturbed Beauty's nod.
Shards cast spirits of sharp light
That dazzled her hooded eyes.

Back at the crumbling castle,
Beauty barred her door and floated

Across her room to the calendar
That drooped on the furthest wall.
She wiped the dust away and stood puzzling
Over the numbers.
A hunt began for the abacus.
She stumbled and prowled about the room,
Leaving trails in her own dust,
Trails she could follow to return
Again and again to the calendar.
The abacus turned up under the bed,
Hiding under mildewed towels
And empty mouse nests.

Click, slide, click.
Slide, click, six months.
Click, slick, clack, three years.
Slick, slack, slide, a lifetime.

Beauty ignored the discreet rapping
At her door
And made her way to the big window.
The curtain fell in a heap
Of rotted velvet as she pulled it back.
The storm of dust coalesced
Into an old friend
Who changed the sheets
And put Beauty to bed.

The moon woke Beauty—
The moon and a starry night—
And more rapping at the door.
Go *away, Wizard*, said Beauty.
Far, far away, Beauty said.
The Wizard of the Wand of Surgical Steel
Stood outside Beauty's door and cast a spell
Of craving.

The door, good and solid and still harboring
Its sturdy dryad,
Threw back that craving spell
Into the Wizard's belly.
But some got through.
Some of that spell
Flew right through the door
And found Beauty.
It found Beauty's belly
And every inch of skin.
It worked a sliver into her brain.

The spell made a fist in her belly.
Right in the center of Beauty
It squeezed and ripped.
It found the pores of her flesh
And puckered them tight.
The sliver worked tunnels
Through her brain.
Beauty paced the room.
Her skirts swirled as she turned in her pacings.
The dust storms kept her company.
She walked the length
And breadth of her room until
She had walked through Pandemonium
And back again.
Then Beauty walked out of the room.

In his study the Wizard shivered
And groaned.
The Wizard in his study growled
And gnashed his teeth as he searched
His rolls of parchment.
He yowled when Beauty spoke.
Time to leave, Beauty said.
Pack up and leave, said Beauty.

You need me, I'm ill, you don't want
Me to go. I'm your friend,
You love me, I'm in charge here!
Roared the Wizard.

The curtains crumbled as Beauty threw
Wide the window.
Parchments lying about the study
Were thrown into the fire by the wind—
Who then teased the Wizard,
Poking other parchments nearer and nearer
To the ones that blazed and
Began to spill
Out onto the hearth.
You're next, said Beauty.
Next to burn, Beauty said,
As the wind played at
The Wizard's robes.
Faster than time the tiny tempest lifted
Up the Wizard and fed him
To the flame.
The wind dusted off its many airy hands
As it blew away through the castle.
When the fire died back,
Beauty cleaned the mess herself.

The urchins rolled back to the sea
Taking most of their spines
With them.

There are new portrait painters,
New Scribes, an Astrologer,
An Astronomer,
And a brave Minstrel or five.
The Executioner has retired

To a part-time job
As a short-order cook.
The Wizard has brethren that blow
Through town
But they only send
Messages
On pretty new parchment
From afar.

Denise Thomas

Notes for an Informal Study
of the Personalities of Tables

Furniture is alive.

The personality of a table is closely aligned with its shape. Tables with corners delight in jumping in the path of hummins fumbling in the dark or those too distracted to notice the actions of a table.

Rectangular tables are all business—functional, conservative. Square tables like fair play. Round tables inspire loyalty, wear adornment well, require the user to adapt to the table. Round tables can comfortably wear from three to six legs.

Tables are fond of doilies and embroidered cloth. Tables gather things: papers, junk mail, keys, glasses, books, pocket knives, lamps, pens, candles, plants, dust and cats. These provide camouflage, a protective facade for the table.

Chewing gum oozes to the underside of tables in restaurants and other public places; this appears to be an adaptive and protection-seeking behavior of the gum. The gum then hardens into barnacle-like structures. It is unknown at present if this is a symbiotic or parasitic relationship.

All tables are altars.

Those tables having only two legs cling to the home, sending tendrils deep into the wood and plaster of a building; the wall becomes a giant limb for the table, regardless of shape. Most tables stand proudly, taking up space without a hint of embarrassment. Even those with delicate, spindly legs perch on their bit of floor haughtily.

Botany Lesson

The cliché, the poetic description;
    the rose of blood
    blooms in the syringe,
    as if the barrel fills with
    paper flowers, suddenly alive.

Truth is much more startling
    than some tiny flower
    opening so delicately.

An amoeba beezzzzzzzzz,
    a crimson hummmingbird,
    eager after refined nectar
    impatient, rushing out
    to wallow in endless honey.

No blossoms
    no leaves
    no roots of red

There's nothing here any longer
    that belongs
    to the poppy.

"Day of the Dead Chair," Mixed Media, Suzanne Manji, 1994, photo by R. H. Hensleigh

Close to the Bone

Suzanne Dolan Manji

The Opthamology Lesson

Dad was alive then. I was three and tiny for my age, but the nurse had to shred a bed sheet to keep me down. She wrapped the linen strips around my abdomen and knotted them under the exam table. Her calculated movements could not outsmart me. I retracted my legs and thrust them forward like a mousetrap when Dr. Upshur tried to get near my right eye. He stared at the nurse in blame and she glared at me. She cut a hole in another sheet and placed it over the bleeding eye and dripped a blurring solution onto my iris. With the good eye covered, they thought they were safe. I slid my eye, the one without the blurring solution, to the hole and knew exactly when the needle was coming. I kicked again. This time they decided to hold me down, my father on one limb, the nurse on the other. I was defeated. I chose the letters E and U and repeated them over and over.

"E-U-E-U-E-U, Daddy, E-U."

My mother had to leave the room. He stayed with me.

I had been running to my pink, plastic secretary desk (the one that looked like *real* wood grain on TV) to get a sugar cube to show Grandma and Grandpa. It was a perfect cube wrapped in satin white with a cardinal on it. I'd slipped on the scatter rug and hit the corner of my mother's favorite marble-topped table. I'd been stunned, but undaunted. Nothing had hurt.

My sister'd come running and screamed, "Suzy's bleeding!"

Then my tears had come. Daddy had scooped me up and taken me to the bare, cream-colored exam room in Poughkeepsie. That's where the ties were bound. I became an artist then, at that moment. The gift of sight became everything. Daddy got me a set of trucks, tiny ones. I used the fieldstones of our porch as states, the grout between as highways. Everything became visual. The relationships of the colored trucks to each other and to the fieldstones, the relationship of my hand to the truck as I moved it around and the fact that I could see it. I got the trucks for being a *good girl*.

I knew better. That nurse shredded the sheets to contain me. I still shred paper. I still use cloth. I still use my eyes.

"The Duende Chair II." Mixed Media, Suzanne Manji, 1997, photo by R.H.Hensleigh

Suzanne Manji

Close to the Bone

That polished rock has a scar, like mine
as close to my eye as a root to its tree.
My memories of you are deep and dark
like that hole where we placed you

up on the hill, beyond the garden
where you and I planted the smokebush
that died, like you, slowly . . . slowly.
A perfect spot, they said, for death.

I remember you swooped me up,
pelican to fish,
on the day I fell and cut my eye
close to the bone.

I was running to get the sugar cube
with the red bird from my pink desk.
Above a rug that scattered me like seeds,
my eye was spared from a cornered table.

You carried me like spring water
to a cold, silver table.
They covered me with cloth
torn to contain me.

Now I know, I need my eyes
for colors and trucks and words
and seeing you leave
on a sunny day
with daffodils falling—
the weight of love and sorrow.

Suzanne Manji

On a metal plate
your name looked strange—
soon to be in polished rock,
your name cut in, like a scar
close to the bone.

Nabeel

He came in July. I'd heard about him before I saw him. Indian. Born in Kenya. A Canadian citizen. Intriguing. I had been drawn to Indian and Eastern things since childhood. Intricate patterns. Flecks of gold. Miniatures painted with a single-hair brush on panels of ivory. Could this explain why I went to such trouble for his arrival?

My co-workers quietly observed my unusual behavior. I dragged a grocery bag into work filled with fresh strawberries (with the stems), a metal bowl, an electric mixer, and a double boiler to melt chocolate. I went for a second trip to the car to haul in Kenya AA whole coffee beans, whipping cream, my Krups grinder, ten of my great-grandmother's hand-painted indigo blue cups, and plastic gold spoons dipped in chocolate. The nurses questioned my sanity. We usually hated when the medical staff fellows arrived because it was a whole new crop to orient to our ways.

The day of the Welcome Coffee, I fussed and arranged the cream and strawberries and napkins and spoons. I called all the nurses into the conference room and they reluctantly waited for the branch chief to bring in the *new guys*. Don entered the room first. He was a sweet-looking fellow from Yale, wearing khaki pants and Hush Puppies. The squishiness of his shoes made him look a little unbalanced when he walked.

Nabeel entered next. His face was exquisite. Gentle bones. Eyes that had seen sadness. His shirt was open exposing a chest full of hair and an African 22K gold chain. I couldn't help staring. He had long eyelashes and dirty fingernails. My mother wouldn't like that. She wouldn't like that his skin was so dark either. This made him very appealing.

He sat next to me and introduced himself. After I told him my name he asked, "What are your plans for the future?" And later, "Will you continue to be a nurse?" and finally, "Are you planning to get an advanced degree?" I was surprised but he didn't seem condescending the way most Washingtonians did when they asked the same questions. He just seemed driven and maybe naively thought everyone was.

Later that summer I told him I was engaged. He didn't react. Later that fall I blurted out that I was obsessed with him. I told him I drove by his apartment on Saturday nights to see if he was home. He didn't react. I broke up with my fiancé anyway.

He asked the other nurses about me. "She seems awfully interested in politics," he said when I flew to Boston for the Democratic Convention. He timidly asked one of the nurses, "She's not a Ted Kennedy groupie is she?"

He kept to himself and I found out why. He believed that he must be five years ahead of where he should be in his career. He couldn't keep ahead and still take time for life. He couldn't go to the beach or travel up north or read a novel for pleasure. He *could* see patients for free and encourage his secretary to apply to college and help *ferners* write papers in perfect English. But he couldn't have a child or renovate a house—"Can you imagine me going to a PTA meeting or Home Depot?" he asked me once.

Sometimes I still wonder what's inside his head. Mystery and wordless thoughts? Neurons sweeping through the fields of science and genetics? He says, "Intuition does not exist, only fact and chemical messengers." But still, the human psyche dwells under that tangle.

Photo by Meteor Photo

"Profile," Oil on canvas, Suzanne Manji, 1994

"Figure," oil on canvas, Suzanne Manji, 1992

Roots and Wings

Suzanne Manji

The day we brought my father's clothes to the funeral home, we stood in the vestibule of Fitzpatrick's. Young Billy Fitzpatrick met us and took the clothes—an ivory shirt, a brown suit, a Countess Mara tie and my father's wedding shoes. My mother said, "It doesn't matter that his shoes are black. You'll only see the brown suit. Otherwise, we will have to put him in his brown shoes." My sister and I agreed with her to keep peace, but we knew he *had* to be buried in his wedding shoes.

Billy Jr. said to us, "Is this everything?"

I said, "Yes."

"Isn't there a wedding ring?" he asked. I fumbled, thinking about the day it was stolen from his finger at the hospital because he couldn't speak to tell anyone.

I said, "No." Billy probably thought we were not giving him the wedding ring because we thought he might steal it. "I wonder why he asked about his wedding ring," I said to my sister Donna. She looked a little greenish.

When Billy had to take care of other business in the kitchen, Donna said, "What can we put in the casket with him?" I thought of the stuffed white bear that my husband, Nabeel, had given me, the bear I slept with when I felt alone. I suggested the bear and Donna wrinkled her nose. I knew the idea was too goofy, too Hallmark.

Donna's eyebrows lifted. She whispered excitedly, "Let's put pennies in his shoes!" It was perfect. I heard the song *Pennies From Heaven* in my head. Then I pictured his silly grin when he used to bring the wedding shoes out to the living room to tease us.

I heard him say, "Yup, I'm gonna be buried in these shoes."

I pictured my Irish grandma, his mother, squealing "Ooooohhhh, nooooo . . . Get those shoes off the bed! It's bad luck." I saw pennies flattened on the railroad tracks by the Hudson river and my coin collection—images all milliseconds apart, like neurons firing. I thought of his saving pennies to take us to dinner and to buy us the things we wanted. We took pennies from our wallets and put one in each shoe. Two girls, two pennies.

Donna whispered, "Don't tell anyone."

Two months after my father died a package arrived, *Priority Mail*. It was from my mother. The melange in one of her packages often included organza ribbon, tiny bouquets of silk roses and one gorgeous treasure unearthed from a garage sale. This box was different. Inside the outer carton was a small stationery box used at one time for envelopes. The box read: *Cougar Opaque, Dynawhite Vellum*. I opened the lid and paused for a moment. The contents were oddly familiar and foreign at the same time. Two Countess Mara ties, a small wooden box with various tie tacks commem-orating events, three yellowed, "humorous" greeting cards, a bullet cartridge from 1943, and a worn leather wallet. My father's belongings. A life gone by. Seventy-two years condensed into this one small box. It reminded me of Lipton Chicken Noodle Soup, with *real* chicken broth. Life and vitality flash frozen and dehydrated and pulverized into an oily glob, 1/24th the size of a live chicken.

The wallet was strange. It held my high school photo, Donna's high school photo, my father's expired driver's license and a small torn piece of paper that read: *Texaco Shares, March 79, 1563 shares*. When my father had entered the VA hospital, he'd often touched his right back pocket for reassurance. After seeing the alarm in his eyes, that his wallet was gone, my mother'd decided to let him keep it. She'd put a five dollar bill in it (knowing it would probably be stolen), a prayer card and his name and hospital unit number. She said with a soft smile, remembering him when he was well, "Daddy always was reaching for his wallet."

He wanted us to have things but never cared much about having things himself. He used one small section of the double bedroom closet and two small drawers in the dresser. Most of his clothes were purchased by my mother because he didn't care much about clothes. He did have a few favorite things though . . . a brown suit, two ties and his wedding shoes. The shoes were black wing tips dated on the inside. They read 1946 in slightly blurred black type. He loved getting them out of the closet to show off that he still had them and still wore them. He especially relished comparing his one pair of dress shoes to my mother's closet full. Hers were all carefully marked with such labels as: *black pumps with silver clips, cranberry velvet wedgies* and *black patent T-straps*.

One item in the box, the bullet cartridge from WW II, was so familiar to me that it had become somewhat meaningless. I had seen it in the drawer of his dresser many times. Nabeel was interested in everything to do with guns, so I decided to show it to him. He was mesmerized by it. He turned it over and over in his hand, puzzled by it. My husband Nabeel's hands were nothing like my father's. Deep olive in color, with black under the fingernails. That bothered me. My father buffed his nails and they were clean and white. I thought I was marrying someone totally different from my father. Indian. Driven. Silly. As it turned out, he was a lot like my father. Every night he came home to the e-mail, a modern day version of the newspaper and the USPS mail. Nabeel then turned on the hockey game. I used to find the sound of sports comforting, but now it interrupted my thoughts. I had watched basketball as a child with my father. I'd pretended to enjoy the game, but what I'd really enjoyed was the sound of him yelling and screaming. He never screamed about anything else. He was logical and didn't ruminate over mistakes. He didn't like arguments or ugly words. Nabeel doesn't either.

I turned my attention to the bullet cartridge. It was an anomaly. I wondered why, with so few belongings, my father would have saved it for fifty-some years. It was brass and copper and was actually quite elegant. Oddly, I heard something rattling. My first thought, about what might be inside, was that it might be a deep, round diamond—put inside for my mother to have if he was killed. Then for some reason, I entertained the possibility that it might be a tooth. My spirits fell when I thought, "Maybe it's just hardened gunpowder."

Nabeel said, "This doesn't look the way it should. It's been sealed with metal—copper." He slowly rotated the cartridge from end to end and listened. I suddenly thought of those metal toys that you hold and try to balance a circular top-like object on the handle. Two spokes, one on either side of the circle, send the top from side to side. I thought of rocking from side to side in a boat. It was hypnotic.

Nabeel whispered, "I wonder what's inside. Don't you want to open it?"

"No," I said quickly. I was afraid of guns and bullets. If we opened it, it might explode in my face.

"What if it's a diamond?" he said. My eyes widened at his

thought. "Or maybe a tooth," he added. I couldn't believe that his thoughts were the same as mine. "Where was your father stationed during the war?" Nabeel gently asked.

"Kwajalein. The Marshall Islands," I answered.

"There was quite a bloody theater there," he said.

"What do you mean theater?" I puzzled.

"Oh, I guess I mean a display. A fantastic display. Like fireworks. Group mentality. It's amazing what men will do in groups," he said.

I pondered this and replied, "My father told me that the Japanese were not afraid to die. He said they would just jump right out into open fire—prepared to be shot dead for their country."

"Exactly. Theater. Hey, maybe it's some Japanese guy's tooth rattling around in there. C'mon, let's open it!" he pleaded.

I squirmed as I thought, "Could my father have taken pleasure in killing—so much so that he would save a dead man's tooth?" He never talked about the war. My mother told me he'd had nightmares for years after he came home.

She said in a whispering tone, "He was a medic and he only had a certain amount of morphine. The soldiers would grab his pant leg and beg for more, many with half their faces shot off. He couldn't give them more pain killer because he needed to ration it so that every wounded soldier in pain would have some. He felt guilty about that."

I thought of the morning that I sat on the back porch steps with my father. I was probably nine years old. He flicked his cigarette butt in the grass, and I ran to get it. I took it and pressed it to an ant on the sidewalk. The ant flipped over and wriggled its legs in a hideous dance.

My father said, "Step on it. Don't let it suffer." He did the same thing when an animal was suffering. Once a dog had gotten hit by a car on our busy street and was breathing hard and rhythmically in the road. When the dog started to seize, my father wrapped it in a blanket and brought it to our yard. He saw the gaping wound and knew it was dying. He called for me to get the shovel while he held the dog. With a swift blow to the head, he killed it. I watched with horror as he carried that dog to the woods and buried it.

Years later my father would, in a sense, have half of his head blown off—but slowly . . . with Alzheimer's disease. I thought about the portrait I had done in art school when I was dealing with my father's slow death. It was a portrait of an older man with his face obscured by smeared paint. That portrait now reminded me of my father. The insidious deterioration of his memories, the annihilation of his function—represented by the smeared paint on the right side of the brain.

My father was a shy man. I rarely remember him talking to anyone except his friend Tony. When he was on the phone with Tony, he came alive. There was a depth and richness in his laugh that I didn't hear at other times. I sighed with relief at his pleasure. He was okay. He was happy for a moment. He rarely seemed happy.

My sister remembered him better. "You only knew him ill— you didn't know the real Daddy," she said.

"Where was he? Who was he?" I wondered. I remembered a quiet man on the couch. A gentle man. A sad man. A man I couldn't talk to.

I remember, as a teenager, sitting across from him at the kitchen table on Saturday mornings when my sister and mother were out shopping. I rearranged my straight hips on the chair several times, clasped and unclasped my hands and tried to start a conversation with him.

"How was the baseball game last night?" I asked in a voice scratchy from silence.

"Okay," he said.

"Who won?"

"New York."

I rearranged myself and said, "Isn't it a perfect day today?"

He answered, "Yup."

I sat, quietly thinking of all the things I really wanted to say to him—things like "Are you okay, Dad?" or "You seem so unhappy, Dad." My eyes welled up with tears and I awkwardly went to the bathroom to blot the wetness away and compose myself. I went back to the kitchen to start the process all over again. My father was now preoccupied with when my mother would be arriving home. He walked from the kitchen window to the front door, watching for her. He seemed to get more frantic with each trip from door to window. The opportunity to have a conversation was lost. Was this his shyness or the beginning of the devastating illness that would take his life twenty years later?

One summer, I decided I was going to get him to talk. I had by now become a psychiatric nurse, and I was going to use my *skills* to get him to open up. I took him for a ride in my new 1980 Honda Civic. We drove in silence.

I finally chirped, "Well, Dad, how do you like the car?"

His long, skinny legs bumped the glove box each time we hit a dip in the road, and he looked uncomfortable. He was probably thinking the car was a death trap.

He said, trying to be positive, "You can really feel the road in this car."

I guessed he didn't think much of it. I decided he needed to talk about his early disability retirement from Texaco Research Center. This was a major life change for him after thirty-nine years, and I determined it was time for him to express his feelings.

I said, "So, Dad, how do you feel about your retirement?"

He looked straight ahead at the road and softly said, "I'd rather be working."

I felt my stomach sink. I felt like a failure. A pompous ass neophyte psychiatric nurse. I wanted to cry. We drove the rest of the way in silence.

O

I remember sitting in the Windsor chair and looking at his brothers while eating lunch the day Dad was buried. I felt so awkward, and I dropped my buttered knife down the side of my dress onto the rug. I felt stupid. His brothers both had that same thick, silvery hair— the hair that gave their father (the barber) the name Whitey.

"Always go to the barber with the bad haircut," my grandpa had said. "The other one cuts his hair." I watched my uncles' gestures, looking for my father. Maybe in their movements or expressions I would catch a glimpse of my father. I didn't. I yearned to hear a story. Something about Daddy. Something funny. I wanted to laugh. I wanted to see him sitting across from me in the living room, on the oak steps that he'd built, and bantering with my great-uncle about the stock market.

My great-uncle would say, "Now Ray, let's just say you had some money to invest. What stock would you buy?" My father, too sharp to be fooled by Uncle Ed's openwork sneakers from Kmart, knew that Great-Uncle was sitting on quite a bundle and ready to invest it based on an educated hunch.

My father read three newspapers every day and had a pretty good idea what stocks were going to respond to critical business decisions discussed in *The New York Times* and *The Wall Street Journal*.

He teased my great-uncle by responding, "Oh, Ed, you know I don't have any money to invest."

My great-uncle got antsy and said, "But let's just say you did."

"No, Ed, I've got the girls in private school, and we need a new car. I just can't invest right now."

Squirming, Ed said, "But Ray, I'm not asking you to invest! This is all hypothetical!"

On and on it went, my father loving every minute of it. He finally broke down and told Ed what to buy, but not without the full enjoyment of the game. After Ed left, my father would say, "Can you believe those shoes? Mesh sneakers? He looks like a pauper. Why, the man could afford anything he wanted! You can't take it with you. It's Mary I feel sorry for. She could be traveling and enjoying life. Instead, she is stuck with that tightwad. I hope he kicks the bucket before she does, so she can at least enjoy some of that money."

He was a generous man. He loved buying us things. Every year we went to Alexander's in White Plains for the big Back to School Sale. He took the day off from work, drove us down and waited in line with all the housewives to get in the store. When the doors were opened, he bolted. He gathered what he thought looked good and what the women were grabbing. He then came to find us and had us hide in a corner and try on the stuff over our clothes while he watched the merchandise to keep it from predators. One year we each got beautiful suede jackets, the likes of which I have never seen since. They were brown and short with detailed pockets and beautiful linings. Smooth as silk. I wore mine till it fell apart and, years later, my mother gave me hers. I wore it to art school every day. It became a totem of sorts and, if I forgot it, I felt like I couldn't paint.

I walked down the hill to our yard from the grave the day of his burial. I thought of his mischievous grin and heard him say to my mother, "Now you just remember—when I die, I am going to be buried right up there on that hill, so I can watch you with your new husband!" Through a strange series of coincidences, she was able to put him right up on the hill in full view of the house. It was possible, I think, because she wasn't planning on any new husband.

I missed seeing him in the garden, bent over the beans and the tomatoes. I missed seeing him come into the kitchen with a rose and saying, "Look, a perfect bud."

I ran back up, despite my embarrassment about what his brother, Uncle Joe, would think, to take one last look at the hole with the long roots coming through the earth. Coming back down the hill, I knew they all thought I was weird or histrionic or false.

"Who cares?" I thought. I'd put something in with him. It was my first tooth. I'd placed it in a tiny copper box that he'd given me when I was a child. I'd dropped it down alongside the casket. He had pulled my baby tooth when I couldn't stand wiggling it anymore. I remember he'd grasped it firmly between his thumb and forefinger and yanked. Before I knew it, the tooth had been in his hand. He'd said, "Don't linger when something hurts . . . get it over with quickly. Slow suffering is far more painful." The molar had "incredible roots," according to my father, and I had saved it all these years because of those roots. When I'd dropped it down into the dirt, next to the casket, I'd been the last one to gape into the hole besides the gravedigger. My yellow dress, the one I'd worn to my art school graduation seven years before, billowed on the windy day. "Shameless. Wearing yellow to her father's burial. She always has tried to stand out," the family said.

○

Exactly one year to the day of my father's death, I decided to open the cartridge. Nabeel had set up this tool that opened cartridges. It looked like a hammer and was ready to be pounded once or twice on a concrete floor or pavement.

I thought, "Leave it to him to have a tool that opens bullet cartridges." I had no idea such a thing existed.

He cautioned, "Remember, once it is opened, you can't seal it back up."

"That's okay," I lied.

I had kept that tool, ready to go, in the closet for what

seemed like months. I took it out. I paced. I went to the bathroom. I smoked a cigarette. I got on the phone. I ate some Valentine's candy . . . I couldn't do it.

The next day the sun melted the pond next to our house, and the temperature peaked at 57° . . . my birth year. It was a sign. Today was the day. Without hesitation, I took the tool to the garage and pounded it in slow, musical tones. Once. No. Twice. No. Three times. No. I talked to myself.

"Hit it hard . . . I'm afraid. What if it explodes? Oh, go ahead, hit it!"

It opened. Two tiny pearls, with golden tones, rattled in the clear chamber. I quickly unscrewed the rubber tip on the chamber and poured them into my palm. They weren't pearls. They were teeth. No, one tooth—broken between the roots. I was horrified. He did save a Japanese soldier's tooth as a trophy. I felt ill. I reeled. I ran through the laundry room from the garage and made it only to the big laundry sink. I wretched and wretched. Tears spilled from my eyes, triggered by what was now the dry heaves. As I tried to clear my vision and regain my balance, my eyes cast down on the tool still in my hand. I noticed a tiny scrolled paper dangling from the open chamber. I wiped my face with cold water and a dirty towel from the laundry basket.

I slowly undid the paper. It was yellowed and intentionally (artfully) burned on the edges. In my father's loopy, messy, heavy-handed script the paper read:

December 31st, 1943

My first tooth,
removed by my father,
Ray Ryan Sr.
in the barber shop
on Mill Street
on June 28th, 1929.

Carry it with you always
for safekeeping.

Suzanne Manji

Don't Go . . . Don't Stay

Right before you disappear
come, on the couch,
and lie
once more

so I can have you
this last time
before you go
inside

I lift my head
and bury it then
like everything else
that was.

One last look
at the roots
on the bottom
before the dirt fills in.

"Daddy," Oil on canvas, Suzanne Manji, 1991
photo by Meteor Photo

The Millionth Snowflake

Nancy J. Henderson

Some Thoughts on How I Write

I descend to the bottom
of Rio Grande Gorge. Volcanic
boulders underfoot, I go
slowly, pick my way through
rock, sage and dirt. I wind
back and forth on erratic
rocky steps, smell fragrant earth
and pine along the way. Terns
call out, *Keep going, keep going*.
My legs ache, and I wonder
how they'll feel climbing back up.

Each pause to rest breathes me closer;
each blade of grass grows lusher
as I near the rushing water.
There is no wondering *if* anymore.
It's just something I have to do.

123

The Photographer

Nancy J. Henderson

Not what I had pictured,
you emerge from the darkroom,
long hair tucked
behind your ears, a face
perhaps too young
for so much gray. I don't
notice how many wrinkles.
But you have noticed mine.

Your camera begins to click
before I have time to focus
on you, on it, on whether
you know what you're doing.
Guardedly grinning, I deceive
the stranger behind the lens;
the fantasies rise from beneath
my lengthy background,
the flash of anxious eyebrows.
Observing the curl in your fingers,
your hair feathering your collar,
the slow cadence to your questions,
I question how much to deny.
Teeth showing, I am vulnerable
to your clicking, your catching
my off-guard moments.

Then it is over, I raise
my glasses to my face,
knowing these photos
might not be to my liking.
But I play along like I don't care.
You'll put them in the mail,
you say. No need to come back.
Your friend brings you lunch,

looks on as you scribble
my address. She is much
too young and shy
for you, you know.

I leave after small talk,
feeling old and wise,
wondering if it will
show in my pictures.

Nancy J. Henderson

Moving

Five o'clock, the afternoon gray
turns grayer as snow begins to fall
sometime after Christmas.
This is the last day I will look
out over the bare willows to the pond
turned white and flat
where ducks convene in icy circles
near the moving water
that won't freeze. Lights begin
to flicker across the marsh
where newer homes went up
last summer. A squirrel
jumps slowly over the deck
looking for handouts. The birds
don't come anymore for his
greediness. Traffic sounds
are muffled on the main road
that winds around the lake
and on into town . . . a small
town I've barely begun to know
as I move beyond the singular
so late in life. Only here
two years, the boxes are
still stacked in the basement,
the aggravation of moving
still fresh in my mind; I listen
to the silence a little longer,
knowing there will be less of it.
The snow falls thicker now
and is the only light of
nightfall. I look to it
to remind me that winter
stays the same,
even as I am changing.

Nancy J. Henderson

Relying on Intuition
and the Millionth Snowflake

Even you believe it's true,
that the frailest of dying emotions
can somehow be explained,
as if it were a snowflake
melting in the sun.

You say it's a synapse,
an electrical path
between two neurons
in the brain. You believe

there's a reason
for everything, even
my clear cloud of anger
erupting from nowhere
when you've ducked my question.

But I have other thoughts
that race around
in thin air, invisible
to the naked brain and
all its electrical circuitry
plugged into this thing
called logic. I've dropped

my thoughts mid-sentence
to reach out for intuition
and yes, I know it to be true,
as true as the millionth snowflake
that is unlike any other.

Nancy J. Henderson

Since You Left for Ruidoso

I don't see anymore. I leave eyeglasses
strewn on the bleached oak kitchen counter,
the pine bedside table. I moved here alone
with my sweaters, cowboy boots and art.
Once a heron flew up into an old elm
and sat awkwardly in view of my binoculars
like a mistake.

In the morning there is the solitude
of one chickadee at a time,
pecking at seeds for sustenance.
I have spaces in this house I haven't
filled and think that I can grow that way.
My bed is large with no one in it.
And then there are the questions
about which birds mate for life.

Nancy J. Henderson

All the Gray

I want you to see as I see,
as big as the sky and more,
as far as the distance
between sun and moon,
and as wide as our differences.
There is no right, out there
between the stars—no wrong
when a comet connects
with the earth. Words fly
around like light and are meaningless
among the angels. What is meant to be
is as simple as a blade of grass
that knows no limits when the rains come.
I am as human as the dragonfly
is insect. We all fly with colors
transparent and deep. There is no
judgment among fuchsias and olives,
no blame among blues for being
so far in the spectrum from reds,
and there is infinite room
for all the truths that lie
between the poles of your thinking
that it must be this way, or it must
be that way. We don't know where it ends
and for all we know, it doesn't.
I want you to see how small we are.
I want you to see.

Nancy J. Henderson

Repacking my Bags

These bags
are synthetic
and hard,
full of
unauthorized smiles.
A natural canvas
is more forgiving
of heavy loads
and washable to boot.
By turning myself
inside out,
I can wash
away memories
of smiles
I would rather forget.
Nobody taught me
the truth
about myself.
I had to find out
the hard way.
Some people
die inside
before they really live.
I leave the bags,
the smiles,
the truth behind,
and travel
with myself now,
a considerably
lighter load.

Parity

Nancy J. Henderson

Among women there are codes
unspoken. Emotions are
set on the table
like plates of cookies
and pots of tea,
trusted to the keeping
of other women.

This does not happen
right away. A little time,
a little talk, a discovery
of who will reciprocate,
a discerning of who will share,
some laughter about the other side,
are first required.

Cookies and tea
become our bread, our sustaining
meal of parity.
Among women there is
a cautious bond, a smile,
a hardship mutually won.

Nancy J. Henderson

Letter to a Friend

We do not see what is. We see what we are.
—Unknown

All the shades of green
reflected in the sun
as that forest rises
from bog are yours,
yours for the seeing.

That deer lying in the road
in springtime, the velvety
fur of what was once
warm-blooded, now gone
to another life, is yours,
yours for the touching.

There are flowers that die,
weeds that grow,
fogs that illuminate,
sunsets that blind.

What if this were all alright?

I cannot help you.
Wild imaginings, like bullets,
fly around in my nightmares,
and I somehow stay free
of the fire. I haven't
any secret. Like you, I would crawl
into a hole with the rabbit
if I could. The sky is
mud or powder, whichever
you want to see.

I can hold these words
out in front of you,
speak them with kindness,
give them breath, but you,
you must love the world
on your own.

Nancy J. Henderson

Reading

One by one
we step up to the microphone,
speak the words
we have solely woven
into a basket of experience.
We hold it forth
to be examined,
acknowledged,
added to a collection
of intertwined words that hold
moments, hours, years
of having held it all in
when there was no microphone,
there was no one listening
for the weave, the container
of one woman's memory.

One by one we finger
the reeds, dip them
in the water of story,
braid them together
in pronounced pattern,
and set them to dry
in the open.

Fog

Nancy J. Henderson

Up close
it isn't there.
It's always
just beyond
the road,
just beyond
the fence,
blocking your view
of beyond.

It lounges
like old snow
over cold dawn
on a January morning
that never quite
becomes day.
It covers you
too soon,
as you try to stay awake
with yawns,
old and wistful.

Nancy J. Henderson

Getting On With It

I never imagined I would be here,
forty years later, this place where
I came for booster shots as a child.
I am here again hoping to free my mind
from all the lies I was taught back then.
I was born with this propensity to faint
at the sight of a needle, the sound of lies.

You sit in a couched room with Venetian blinds,
smiling at clients as they enter.
You read fear on my face, but that's not it.
I have overcome my fears. Now
I build walls for you to tear down
as you too tell me the needle won't hurt.

Is that a lie?
I suffer from congestion,
digging in my bag for Kleenex,
throat lozenges, water.
What have I brought here?
A teddy bear, sand castles,
some chocolate hearts that melt.
I have no sunglasses, no hat,
no shame at what I have become.
I am not a child anymore.
I have watched the seasons come and go
many times now
and they are never
as predictable as I am.

Put the needle down
so I can recover on my own.

Nancy J. Henderson

Re-creating

These Sangre de Christo mountains
smell like dust and juniper,
look like the mountains
of emotion inside me
I have yet to climb.
The dead wood, rock,
sage, pine, and mesquite
roll over my heart, as I sit
on a skyline, in the middle
of this painting I have
yet to create, on a June
afternoon.

This dirt, this air smell old
and familiar as the childhood
I left behind. I return
to where I was then,
to blend with the earth
that nourishes me.

I stroke the tips of imagined brushes,
gaze into lavender, fuchsia, rose,
but can't seem to mix the colors
with my own precarious palette.

I climb into my childhood,
remembering how it felt
to be close to my senses,
close to my innocence,
connected to my landscape.
I reach to touch a cactus,

remind myself it is not a dream.
I was that child once.
I can be her again, see her
like this landscape, this painting
that is unpainted. Pulling old colors
from inside, I give birth
to myself everyday.

Daylilies

Nancy J. Henderson

If only it were all this simple,
the long, thin leaves rising
out of dry earth, mid-summer orange
or yellow standing amid the forage,
stark and pointed as honesty.
If only we were all so clear
as a roadside brush of color
that survives even the cruelest
drought, or soaking storm,
to unfold again once more.

In winter it is a bulb
lying round, poised
to begin again. Spring
directs its soul to renewal,
the optimism of every cycle.
A daylily recognizes even the smallest
rain drop, welcomes any and every
hardened beetle. Life is rooted
in this soil and death
becomes this bloom
that is so innocent, it will
always come back again.

Nancy J. Henderson

Starting Out

Just in case you thought
you knew me,
I'm going to sleep
on the windowsill tonight
where the crickets
will sing my lids heavy.
I'll shiver in a pink dress
that's painted with wildflowers.
Just in case you thought
you knew me,
I haven't ironed your shirts
or remembered to buy the milk.
The day got away from me
when I noticed sunlight
on a spider web outside
the back door.
Just in case you thought
I was the same woman
you fell in love with,
I won't shave my legs anymore
or leave the light on the porch.
I'll read history until daylight
and kiss you in the morning
before you've awakened.
And when winter comes
the snow will mount up
on the sidewalk
and I'll make tracks
in pursuit of a longer day
when I'll have time to tell you
over and over
that I'm not
who you thought
I was.

Unveiled

Nancy J. Henderson

I want to marry in suede,
the soft side of an animal's hide,
connected to the earth
a creature of the wild.
No white or lace, no veil
of diaphanous masking.
No make-up or pretense.
I am eyes that are naked,
open to the possible.
There is no knowing.
Tomorrow brings seasonal change.
Animal sharing is skin to skin,
toe to toe, one on one survival.
Coupled for life we will protect
each other, lie together
through the thick of it,
with no question.

I'll hold a bouquet
of wild flowers
in front of the warmth
of a fire, leave you space
to be you. Touching toes to kiss,
our feet are on the ground
in leather boots, removed
at the door of our life
together.

Down Deep

Nancy J. Henderson

I walk with padded feet
across the paper, step down
deep for what's underneath.
What is this ground I tread,
what is this earth made of?
Buried under my footsteps
are perhaps artifacts, ideas
never noticed or regarded
as valuable. I walk slowly,
in meditation, feel the rising grass,
feel the growth of thoughts
that could voice what it is to be
human on this earthly sphere;
a speck in this galaxy with black holes
that devour stars and universes;
a speck on a thin, white sheet
that signifies my existence.
I am so small, so big, so padded
by this paper, so unbalanced
on these feet that tread
a spinning planet.

Uprising

Barbara Shooltz Kendzierski

Uprising

Pulling myself back
up, still grounded
in dark mud, rich earth
balanced secure
in feeling sustained
I rise, rise up
through my toes, my ankles,
through my knees, my pelvis;
shoulders roll back, chin lifts;
in my thoughts
within my heart
woven through
all of my being
my soul rises
into voice.

My Sons

Barbara Kendzierski

for Peter and Michael

You did not come to me
as the moon, reflective
of me, to orbit my life
but as the sun, radiant
with light and warmth
and path of your own.
I will try always
to remember.

I want neither to hold
you captive to my dreams
nor to pressure you to color
between lines I have drawn.
I hope never to distort your questions
to fit my answers; but sometimes
I will forget.

May the limits I set serve you
like a scaffold serves the skyscraper
in its ascent, then falls away
when the time comes to let go.

May I be a mirror
so you see yourself clearly
as child of a loving God
who delights in your being.

And may my words
teach you to listen
and my listening
teach you to speak,
so in quiet it is
your own voice you find.

Barbara Kendzierski

Walking the Dog

It is a painful lesson,
this learning when to let go,
when to release a futile
hope of being heard, like
the day I took Fella for a walk.

We matched pound for pound
but with his four legs to my two
Fella held an advantage.
I held the leash.

I savored a delicious authority
as we toured Macomb Street,
Fella and I at our tug-and-pull tempo.
Not even those despised red Mary Janes,
baby shoes I called them,
could diminish my five-year-old poise.

We made a fine pair,
the Shepherd mutt and his mistress,
until the gray squirrel on Mrs. Buck's
front lawn flicked its tail
in a challenge my charge
could not ignore.

Fella shot down the sidewalk
and up the elm
with me in tow like a soup can
on a speeding wedding car,
my *Stop, Fella! Stop!* drowned out
by his barking commands.

My mother asked the obvious question
as she gently cleaned the grit
from my bloody face and knees:
Why did you hold on?

147

Barbara Kendzierski

Soul Garden

Karen protests
she is no gardener.
I know better.
I chanced a glimpse
of her garden today.
Suspended by ribbons
in a shelter for women,
her hand-painted banners
bloom in shades of spring.

Though Karen seeks solace
in her own dark room
battered by winds
of her soul's fierce storm,
her banners blossom
in witness to hope—

as bulbs, once silenced
in winter's grip and
worn raw by pressures
of freeze and thaw,
now rise in iris
tulip daffodil choir,
raise their faces to the sun,
and lift their voices
to sing in the light.

Barbara Kendzierski

The Little Engine That Could

Epilogue

After her journey over the mountain
pulling the train filled with good
things to eat and wonderful toys,
The Little Blue Engine returned
to her post switching trains in the yard.

Over the years when the big engines
were busy, The Little Blue Engine
had other adventures chugging
and puffing her *I think*
I can, I think I can song.

Now when she is asked to travel over
the mountain, down into the valley
or across the long, flat plain,
her answer is usually, *Yes, I think*
I can, I think I can, but sometimes
she says, *No,*

for she has learned over her miles
of track, this Little Blue Engine That Could,
while most times she can, it's okay
if she can't, and she does not always
have to do it alone.

Barbara Kendzierski

Laundry Lesson

Any Betty Crocker Homemaker of Tomorrow
will tell you, if she's worth her salt,
you have to know how to sort.
Here the rules are ultra
clear. Those little labels in the seams
shout them out for you: *warm wash,*
cold wash, machine wash,
hand wash, hang dry, tumble dry,
dry flat, dry clean
and *non-chlorine bleach when needed.*

You can have it all—
bright dark
white color
delicate sweats—
if you respect the need to spin
in separate loads.

So, listen to your labels.
Segregate your darks and lights
or lose them all to dingy gray.
Beware of new denim on high—
its blues can ruin your load.
Never let sweat socks take a tumble
with Victoria's Secret lace panties and don't
overload your drum.

Barbara Kendzierski

Summa Cum Laude

She used to be important.
She used to wear
important clothes
and carry important
papers in her briefcase.
Officers and directors
sought her advice.
She used to preside
over conference calls from
her big-city office
with the waterfront view.
Her business card identified
her: *Attorney-at-law*
in a silk-stocking firm
as old as Michigan.
It used to be easy to know
who she was.

Then one summer day
she drove away
from the office and
decided not to return—

now, with no card she
lives undefined. Some days
when she feels too naked
her mind takes her back
to the sleek office tower where
she strides through the lobby
impatiently checking her watch,
so it is obvious that
someone important is
waiting, someone who
knows her by name.

Barbara Kendzierski

Driving Blind

I escape to sleep, crouch low,
elusive as a shadow in the darkness.
But the couriers are clever. Like town criers
their voices clang at every corner.

A shiny chrome toaster with classic lines
stands disabled on the counter,
levers broken off.
I try in vain to reconnect.
I cannot control light
or dark or up or down.
Valves fail on the fish tank. Overflowing water
sweeps the fish into grocery store aisles.
Here they are, aisle 7, canned goods.
Fish mouths freeze in a permanent gasp,
fish eyes appeal to Libby and Del Monte
but their efforts are fruitless.

At the office
without an electronic keycard
I am forever exiled
in the stairwell. Steps are missing.
One slip and I will plummet
nine floors to certain death.
The office manager says if it's this hot
tomorrow, we can all wear
cotton underwear. Excavators

arrive in the neighborhood.
My house is next to be destroyed but I can't leave;
my clothes don't match. The house lists
like a sinking ship; as the tide rushes in, I pull
three gray-haired ladies to the door.
Relieved they are safe, I can relax
and drown, but the toddler in church

won't let go of my arm. Her saddle shoes clunk
on the wooden pew, so I carry her
back to the vestibule.
She clings to my leg; she thinks
I'm her mother. So does the duck

who hatched in my closet.
Though he now wears men's clothes
he still looks to me to be fed.
Feeling like Judas I lure him
to the facade of a home
and dump water on his head.
He splutters then discovers his wings.
The staff discusses delusions
and refers him to marriage counseling
even though he's single; it is standard practice.
As they lead him away he is calm;
he now knows he's a duck.

The staff members aren't ducks
so they fail to see the possibility.
I cry to see him go.
The hospital is closing,
the parking lot lonely and dark.
Frightened, I ask the security guard
to walk me to my car.
When he smiles I see his fangs.
I am the passenger in a car with no driver.
As I grab for the steering wheel
it dissolves. In the fog I drive
blind in frantic search
for quiet.

Death Interrupted

Barbara Kendzierski

I live a Lazarus life,
a death interrupted,
foiled by *effective*
intervention.

The resident on call dictates
for insurance purposes:
Formulation—conflicts
involving desire to die,
yet longing to live.

We make a pistachio cake
in OT today. Six of us
take turns folding
Jello pudding into Cool Whip.

Later in group,
they tell us to be positive
and assertive but not aggressive,
then lead us to the dayroom for meds.

I hear the click
of double doors
at the corridor's end
locking the world out.

After lunch trays are cleared
two frightened student nurses
ask me to play Scrabble.
How can I explain
the words are all used up?

Saturnalia

Barbara Kendzierski

Child of Saturn
celebrate the harvest.
Sing silent praise
for the dying season.
See the black sun rise,
sol niger eclipsing the soul.

Feel the numbing
cold rays beat down
on belief and burn into its roots
until, at last, truth lies
in the unknowing—
like chaff in the field,
the essential remains.

By Design

Barbara Kendzierski

Creatures speak in sounds.
The word of God is silence.
—Simone Weil

Why did you let me down?
Why didn't you catch me
when I lost my balance?
I shattered on impact.

Your hand created
this clay as it was,
not perfect but solid,
seamless, smooth.
I once stood tall.

Why didn't you break
my fall?

I have waited too long
for your hand to restore me,
to make me whole.
In your silence
I struggle to gather
the scattered shards,
to reclaim the form
I have lost
but the fragments,
each its own jagged
design, refuse to fit
the mold.

Fingering chips of clay,
I start to arrange them
in new, whimsical ways,
leave space in the contours
for those yet to be
found. Shadows take
shape in the crackled
glaze; like grout
they fill the gaps.

In this textured melange
I create in your quiet
a mosaic begins
to emerge;
so it is
I shatter
toward wholeness.

Duet with my Grandmother

Barbara Kendzierski

for Ellen Mahony Shooltz
1898-1976

June 22, 1997

I sit at her mahogany dressing table,
now my desk, and wonder if she too
rested her pen on this wood, pausing
to reflect or to dream.

>   *March 5, 1939*
>
>   *My heart is lonely here tonight,*
>   *These rooms so large and still appear.*
>   *Though their charm and comfort seem to be*
>   *Offering warmth and sympathy*
>   *Why to their friendliness and cheer*
>   *Am I so unresponsive?*

So many treasures she gave me—
her golden locket, her silver mirror,
the pink china angel she said looked
like me, and the small gray box of her
poetry written in graceful script.

>   *Perhaps because last night a blustering North wind*
>   *Bore feathery white clouds and dressed up in state*
>   *Each castle and cottage, each field and street*
>   *And robed them, ermine-clad, royal and great.*

I knew her as an explorer
of Southwestern deserts, an artist
with yarns, a generous woman
with a curious mind, wisdom
and quick Irish wit.

158

This task completed, the North wind withdrew
His icy breath afar from our reach;
As folks, young and old, their windows looked through,
A different version was mirrored for each.

She was a grandmother of surprises, like
the tiny first bra (more like two little
doilies), lacy and white,
she sent from Tucson for my
First Communion.

Children saw sleds, toboggans and skis,
Snow forts and battles, snow angels and sheep;
Mothers saw need for mufflers and gloves,
Rubbers, galoshes, yes and porches to sweep.

But there is another woman I know
only through her poems—the young
wife stunned by her husband's death,
suddenly a young mother alone.

Dads saw walks to be shoveled again;
The car may be stuck in a snowdrift or two.
But I, all alone with my thoughts unrestrained,
A symbol of Death beheld in the view.

I have heard that while the funeral
procession slowly left the church
the village of Chesaning stood still
to mourn, with her and her lad,
the loss of a remarkable man.

Here was Earth's brow quite rigid and cold
Folded so calm neath its snowy white sheet,
Not a bird to be heard nor a beast to behold,
The desolate picture was ghostly complete.

When she writes of the *joyful sorrow*
of loving and losing a man so fine,
her grief glistens in verse
like ice crystals on pine boughs
after a late winter storm.

> *But I know when tomorrow the sun returns*
> *The snow in wee rivers will flow neath the trees,*
> *Birds and squirrels will visit my feeder while*
> *The bough where it hangs will swing in the breeze.*

Though the pages yellow and grow fragile
with age, the strength in her voice
will not fade; it echoes within
the healing pulse of Creation. Here
her legacy I hold . . .

> *And I know before long will the buds swell and burst*
> *And the grass blades push up through each earthly clod.*
> *'Twill be spring, 'twill be Easter, resurrection morn,*
> *Through nature I envision resurrection with God.*

Barbara Kendzierski

Mar 5, 1939

My heart is lonely here tonight;
These rooms so large and still appear,
~~Though~~ their charm and comfort seems to be
Offering warmth and sympathy,
Why to their friendliness and cheer
　　Am I so unresponsive?

~~(Perhaps because)~~
~~Last~~ a flattering
~~night~~ wind from ~~off~~ the North
Bore feathery white ~~snow~~ and ~~clothed~~ dressed up in state
Each ~~castle~~ girl cottage and field and ~~each~~ street
As~~robed~~ like ~~the~~ ermine-clad royal and great.

This task completed, the ~~north~~ wind withdrew
His ~~old~~ icy breath afar from our reach
And ~~folk~~ ~~their windows~~ looking through
And a different version was mirrored for each

The children saw sleds, toboggans and skis
And snow forts, and b ~~wheels,~~ ~~and sheep~~
And mothers saw ~~need~~
And rubbers, galoshes ~~eep~~
And dads saw the ~~in~~
And ~~mayhap~~ the car may be stuc
But I, all alone with ~~ep~~
a symbol of Death

For Here was Earths bro
And folded so calm ~~heet~~
Not a bird nor a b ~~to be seen~~ ~~to sti;~~
The ~~picture of death~~ ~~desolate poster~~

Barbara Kendzierski

Postcard from the Lobby
of Detroit Receiving Hospital

I soar on my swing
arch my back, stretch
my legs eager to tap
my toes on the clouds.

I don't need your labels
and diagnostic assessments—
flat words with no
fizz for what bubbles
inside. You're missing the fun.

The minutes are dancing,
the sunflowers smell
sweet in their beds.
I smile with strangers
(who aren't really strangers).
I laugh with syllables

and wink at kites
sailing over my head.
Plaques on the wall
sing of Swahili
and Triton,
constellations of heaven
and indigo blue. Easter grass
sprouts in its peacock
blue bedpan; purple
pansies and daisies
spring up in applause.

A blood red cardinal
studies our species
through glass
as the female urinal

gives birth to a bundle
of carnations and freesia,
garnished with fern.
My book of seedlings squeals,
the pen tickles its ribs,
and the man in sequined shorts
sips his soda from a dinosaur's head.

I see coy ivy flirt with the doctor's
knee. The boxy white planter
edges its way to the door. They
know the sky is blooming
and fandango can wait.

Born of Night

Barbara Kendzierski

Creator of the world . . .
destiny's fiery Mother . . .
you alone give birth.
—Orphic hymn

In my stillness waiting
unrushed as in the womb
afloat in emptiness
and engulfed by darkness,

new layers of being unfold;
senses ripen, strengths evolve
to grasp, to trust in their fullness
to grow beyond the boundaries
until, without warning,

my world seizes me, crushing me
where I once was nurtured and safe;
I am now battered by crashing waves,
severed to face a journey
I did not choose.

What was familiar looms
foreign and fierce;
unrelenting pressure destroys
all I thought I knew.

With lungs seared by frantic
gasps in newness
I cry, *Why*
do you abandon me?

Barbara Kendzierski

Creation groans her answer
with the pain of her labor;
straining, contracting
she opens, eager
for birth
she stretches
to embrace her own . . .

"Splashdance—Michael at Port Elgin" Peter Kendzierski, 1997

"Searching for Signs," Stephanie Matthews

Living by Definition

Stephanie Matthews

Nature's Revision

On Old Mission Peninsula, the trees close in, wrap shadows around 40-ouncers of Black Label. Lake Michigan pounds onto the shore and gathers those broken beer bottles. As I walk the beach, stop and make sand angels, I stumble upon pieces of polished beach glass—frosted green and amber—the waves' reproduction.

Driftwood sculptures protect me from the sand spiders; crooked-necked giraffes, lopsided blue herons guard my sanctuary. The sound of my bare feet running on the ripples of sand as I hurdle the washed out castles. My footprints sink into the wet beach, fill with water, leave lakes, small traces of me. Just like when I write words with rocks. Words like water shape the beach, re-create glasses of wine, deliver symbols of sand dollars.

The sandhogs are busy building tunnels underwater, elevated structures of steel. I sign my name on the sand with a stick, as the wave arches and breaks onto shore.

Riverwalking

Black ice slides into Manistee River
where backsides of buildings waver in water's cold darkness.
Night lounges about like cats on a couch.

We follow ghost bums
who crouch under this bridge
guzzle bottles of Mad Dog
and scrape packed dirt from under their nails
with broken twigs
they find next to the frozen pancake
dropped by a scared mutt.

We cross the bridge toward the window with the red light,
to find it is only the Smuggler's Cove Saloon
and not the room with whips and pineapple rings
where people meet to make wet monkey love.

Through glass we watch
a crowd of country hicks with identical hair
and Kmart plaids
dance off-beat to Ted Nugent's *Fred Bear*.

Past the bar,
a shack with stairs leads to a chained door.
We rattle the links to scare away those shadows
hiding behind that twisted crabapple tree,
rust chunks drop down to the half a dock

which buckles toward the seaweed fish,
caught over and over by fishermen mistaking the snag for a bass,
then frantically reeling in the dead weight
in hopes of a pike.

Under the stairs is a patio chair,
the faded blue seat cloth torn on the side.
We rest and take turns sitting in it,
wondering why, in this run-down place,
claustrophobic of gray,
there's a bright green plastic garbage can
with a bumper sticker reading: *Vote Republican*.

Stephanie Matthews

The Cabins on Chief Lake, Norwalk, Michigan

Follow me down the cabin road
and I'll show you the pennies,
now flat and faceless,
stuck to the train tracks with toothpaste.
With your ear to the track you can hear
the train, just like the sea
in a shell. Down by the lake are the snail
castles circled by moats of minnows.

The pale yellow cabin is my grandma's.
Inside, smells of pancakes and sausages float by,
and grape juice in frosted glasses. Molasses cookies for dessert.
After half an hour we can swim to the raft, jump
on the big, black whale balloon and flip off the highdive.
Or we can go fishing. Take the rowboat down
to Pudgies Point and cast a few among the lily pads.
Beware of the Chief Lake Monster,
this giant snapping turtle overturns boats.

Darkness encircles the purple bug
zapper and the sauna awaits. Steam rises
from the pot-bellied stove as its hot metal skin
cracks and blisters in a rusty rage.
Remember heat rises as you choose
one of the three wooden benches to sit and sweat.

Take three fast steps down to the lake and dive in,
but watch out for the muskrat that hides under the raft;
he's not as friendly as the bluegill that nibbles your toes.
Quick. Grab your towel and come stand by the campfire.
Grandpa is telling stories of his days on the railroad.
That's how he lost his eye you know.
A piece of flint still
sticks there.

On the railroad, he once cut off a man's foot
so the gangrene wouldn't spread. That story, though,
isn't as popular as the one about digging up Aunt Eunice's hand.
If you're lucky he'll even tell the one about the cat in the cream,
how Mr. Modine flung that drowned cat clear across Norwalk.

If we had more time I could show you a thing or two
about horseshoes and gutting fish,
the sweetpeas and the Chocolate Drop,
but the cabins have disappeared,
Grandma and Grandpa have died.
You will never be able to find the road again.
Next time you look it will be paved and private.

Spooning

Stephanie Matthews

It creeps in and plops down,
straight out on this Sunday afternoon,
a stack of questions
mosquito-biting my mind.
Happiness can only exist inside a moment.
Biking trails with Vince at 2:30 am,
screaming up hills steep and black,
riding against hope, toward fear.
Or in his Mustang on I-94, at 140 my face pulled
taut out the sunroof as we turn to Lake Michigan.
Skinny-dipping at Blackmear Beach
that flashlight chasing us naked over stone walls
we run past Manfred's mansion, the Mafia king of Bridgeman,
and shut our ears to the Doberman ghosts
howling behind trapped doors.
But my claim for dangerous adventures
is shadowed by needs for stability;
quiet harmony, sure to bring boredom,
dangles just behind a shower curtain, caked with mildew
but nevertheless—familiar.

The questions persist
into Monday morning, spooning with Sanjay on the couch,
his right arm wrapping itself over me,
but this ten minutes of happiness will only last until lunch.
And then I muddle time with people and phone calls
because I'm afraid to be alone.

To know that every morning
I must wash down three spiders before showering—
that is comfort, yet I slip farther away from control
and that's when I look myself in the mirror
and the image stays as I fade into the corner of my basement
where chalk drawings on the cement wall jump into each other,
traced hands; my brother, me, my mom, big, bigger, biggest.
And do you think she knows? Did Mom find the key buried,
while she was mushrooming for morels, down by the swamp,
as she dug through marriage, death and kids?

I grew up on a dead-end road in Norwalk, Michigan,
where a shot of peppermint schnapps and a hunk
of pickled bologna made you healthy, wealthy and wise enough to
know the speckled crappie in Chief Lake really can hear you.
It was here that I learned to duck beneath an underpass
and lift my legs over railroad tracks.
And that song, *A Diggy-Liggy Li & A Diggy-Liggy Lo,*
I Don't Know Which Way to Go still
seeps out my lips.
I want to go back to 8905 Lyman Road,
spread out my childhood on our linoleum floor
and throw it away piece by piece.

Stephanie Matthews

The Spoons that Feed Us

Melby Mordig.
Red-orange hair strands flopped over his squinty eyes
as he crouched in the corner of Mrs. Kahl's third-grade class.
Melby Schmelby, the class chanted.
His laugh-it-off smile quivered as he stared hard
into wooden gouges.
Burnt sienna freckles, too many to be cute,
he'd sit on the portable steps at recess with Meda.

Meda Wolfe.
White strangles of hair pulled away from thick black glasses
that slipped off her nose.
You're so ugly your daddy couldn't love you, they'd tease.
Then Meda would pee her pants.
Bright yellow urine trickling down her polyester slacks.
If she only knew Garanimal clothes brought friends.

And were the few of us who sat quietly, not joining in,
thankful that we weren't the victims, any better?
Thirty-year-old women and men
are sitting in front of an Oprah audience,
sobbing for the name-calling,
the humiliation of childhood.

Stephanie Matthews

Working Eulogy

Streetlights pool on wet pavement
as night plops down like the old man on the bus
who could be anyone's grandfather.

Every night he staggers into the very last seat,
rides the route through, hands me his brown bag
and says nothing I haven't heard before.

My grandfather
probably had dreams and aspirations
before the sterilizing period.

Yes, alcohol kills germs,
works well with honey and lemon to fight a cold
and erects walls bigger than Pink Floyd could ever imagine.

And sitting under the dark side of the moon,
I stare straight up the dying pine.
What shall I say?

Shall I say that he meant well
hiding his whiskey in tall, iced tea glasses,
that forgiveness is Christian and sign me up?

Part of me tries really hard to find those good memories,
wrap them with tissue paper and place them in a shoe box for a
rainy day when my kids ask about their great-grandfather.

It's like erasing a chalkboard with a dirty eraser.
It was easier when I was just angry.
Now twenty-five, looking back to four,
it's nearly impossible to link those two ages.

When I was four, he was my grandpa
who pushed me on the rope swing,

told me, *Keep your nose clean,*
every Christmas hung a special stocking just for me.

Now, he's *Grandfather*
because the detached formality of words
makes the dissection digestible.

But you see, Robert C. Williams is still living
and I write his obituary, searching for something
I can't quite find.

Time slips between couch cushions
as I crawl up on the lap of forgiveness,
and listen closely for a pulse.

Stephanie Matthews

Pandora's Box

The key is hidden
inside the plaid footstool
that Melvin made. This
blind man, Melvin, was always
constructing things, touching
not only the smooth
surface but also underneath
where it is dark. I slide
my whole arm into the hollow
stool, reaching for the gold key.
Melvin said my mom was his eyes.
I read that when a patient receives
a cornea transplant, she sees
what the dead person sees.
Mom is the world's seeing eye dog.

Her sister Sanie, now 43, sees as a six-year-old.
I hated Sanie for being retarded.
Mom has scars on her arms from Sanie's digging.
I was embarrassed by her polyester and repeated:
How you doing? How you doing? How you doing?
I still don't know the answer.

I think I've found the key
stuck in the corner, but my fingers
won't reach. I pound on the side
to free it. The key
slips into my palm.
So long since I've seen it,
the end is tarnished but the top

still beautiful. Two flower designs
coming together, then splitting into the
shaft.

My brother is in Sault Ste. Marie
studying how to be a cop and in control
of us. It's too bad,
he's good with kids. He should be a teacher.

The box sits on a high shelf in the kitchen
where it cannot be seen or reached without
the footstool. I rub the dust away with
an old T-shirt Sanjay left months ago
when we were engaged.
Now separated by culture, religion,
and my desire to be free and alone
without boundaries,
I miss him.
Still I am not happy.

I forgot how heavy the box
is, swirled in black and gold
with little red-eyed fish swimming
into each other. On top lies the pink
and purple striped pillow laced with black
fringe and a seed pearl in the center.
I'm afraid to open it.

Mom gave me a pink teddy bear when I was six
and I named him Fuzz Buzz. I didn't know
she was on her way to the hospital to deliver
her dead baby she had carried for nine months.
He died on February 14 and she delivered on March 20.
My brother Daniel was born a year later.
He has eleven fingers and I have twelve. Perhaps those fingers
are reminders of what we leave behind and the extras we take on.
Fuzz Buzz still holds my tears.

It's not just what the box holds that frightens me,
but what it doesn't. The things I have yet to place inside.
Pearl S. Buck once said, *Every great mistake*
has a halfway moment, a split second
when it can be recalled and perhaps remedied.
My mistakes are many.

I turn the key over and over in my hand,
knowing it's too late:
the box has already been opened.

Stephanie Matthews

Searching for what I Believe

Sanjay's sister Shallu fries *paranthas*
for breakfast,
serves tea to her *Dadigee*
out of respect for family.

I look around my cluttered room
and long for space. Shallu
understands the importance
of people.

In India, time stands still.
People come and go, to market
to buy hot pink *saris*.
The days go on just like last year.

I believe in simplicity,
the way an Indian woman
applies blush with lipstick,
buys fabric in the market,
tailors her suits to fit
morning and night.

Painting Spaces

Stephanie Matthews

The tree spreads out,
flat and honest across the water-papered landscape.
One arm invites its dark reflection
from the window pane. Below
the shadow grows short,
afraid to move farther from its beginning.
Just outside my window the tree stands
alone and braces against winter's wind.
The branch scratches at my window,
the tree firmly rooted to earth, yet reaching.

Stephanie Matthews

Universal Prescription: Desire

You know me like the bottom of your bathtub
cold and slippery, yet inviting.
Close to you as your flannel sheets
warm and disarrayed.

I will never leave.
I'm the ache in the pit
of your stomach,
undeniable urge
to brush all clutter of happiness aside
and embrace the fog.
To only dream of sailing the world
is to eat Pez to stave off hunger.

Look at your hands. The palms
are your future, the backs your past.
A crowded commune of lines.

Crazy Joe told you marriage wards off
loneliness so you found someone.
Was that your longing or just a step
to the white picket-fenced mirage

because the loneliness persists
into those hours between 2 & 4 am?
Crouching beside the coffee table,
you search for answers.

When you smell the ocean, it is I,
salty on your lips. You reach
for the glass of water;
it is empty.

Learning by Definition

Stephanie Matthews

Sex is an art, love is a chore.

Affair, light and airy, the word floats between wanting and needing. Never lurking like Adultery, harsh and final—forever a commandment.

The tongue while kissing tries to be faithful, to escape past the body to a still lake in the middle of the woods. Surrounded by locusts on a hot day and grasshoppers on a cool night, there is peace. But the answers seldom come through the tongue. Yogis say intelligence comes through the toes. Sliding the foot down around legs, smooth to rough, lovers know the difference.

The hands gather flesh, smooth back hair, lead the fingers in and out, linger long enough to trace the inner ear. Listening for a cue, the breath once short and tapered now flows as dew on dandelions—the soft bright yellow rubbed on knees to find out if you like the opposite sex. Graduating to daisies, "He loves me, he loves me not," sung by girls wanting boys. They tear off petal after white petal needing to end with love. Quickly they learn to forget the mind and leave the heart and its strings. See sex as simple pleasure. Bodies become tools to get what they want. Balancing between bed sheets, they find the answer.

Stephanie Matthews

I Told Him my Name was Lola

The orange-white Taco Raunche sign blurs down
to the Playdoh green dashboard as I drive this Dutchman home
from Rick's Cafe.
Heavy with accent, full of tequila, his words slosh around
something about soccer coaching in Portage.
Oh yeah? I say. *Cool.*
Never mind the question, those words fit everything this night.

Reaching his house, he kisses me, thanking me for the ride
so I take him to this cornfield, throw down the blanket
from my trunk and find out what a French kiss is
to this man from Holland.
Isn't this illegal in Michigan? he keeps asking
as if there is a chance I'll call the cops
for such a friendly overseas gesture.

Rolling around in hours, as the July night holds its breath,
the low hum of locusts hovers above as I slide my fingers
down between shoulder blades; tongues loll in mouths
and search simple differences.
I don't look into his eyes
instead at the seven dark condos, empty replicas of one another,
black picket-fenced yards with their token shade trees. Weeping
willows hang like tails of horses.

I turn into his gaze
and he says, *This is nice,*
and I don't even care.
I just rub up against him the way so many others have done to me.
Ice-scraped skin numbs out its own pain.
Now I appreciate the shadowed separation of mind
and body as I lay naked tan beside him.

I smooth his chest hairs with my tongue,
cover him with the ratty blanket and drive home alone,
fixed to the frogs jumping on top of each other
under the persistent glow of my headlights.

Stephanie Matthews

Men for Sale

My collection of men, ready for their dusting,
sits proudly on top of my bookcase.
I rearrange them every morning, and every night choose one to
sleep with—
they are more fun than teddy bears. I yank the cord
between their legs to make them talk.
Some are battery-operated, others come with sticks.
Sticks pushed in their backs force them to dance
to anything by the Flaming Lips.

These men with tiny testicles emit just enough testosterone
to relax me, except for the new guy.
This arrogant blue-light special, full dimples, top to bottom,
is trouble.

He leads a charge
of little marching men around my head chanting:
I don't know but I've been told, a big-legged woman
ain't got no soul.

So I gather them up and toss them into a shoe box.
And there they will stay, covered with tissue paper
until tomorrow's garage sale.

Stephanie Matthews

Before Letting Go

Before letting go of lovers
you must smell them
one last time
while they sleep next to you,

for as time curls under itself
like yesterday's carrot peelings,
smells linger the longest
like Limburger cheese.
Even death smells.

Before letting go of an object
you must study it
touch below the surface
bite it
if it's an apple   crawl inside
the worm hole and taste
the juices drip

                  drip

                          dripping between your lips.

Before letting go of him
look into his eyes glazed by promises
you didn't deliver.
See closely the birthmark on his right hip
and notice how the lines have changed without you.

Listen to his breath rise and fall with the rain.
Nuzzle your head upon his arm
kiss that belly button
trace those caterpillar eyebrows with your fingers
whisper *Shukria*°
and don't look back.

° Hindi word for *thank you*

187

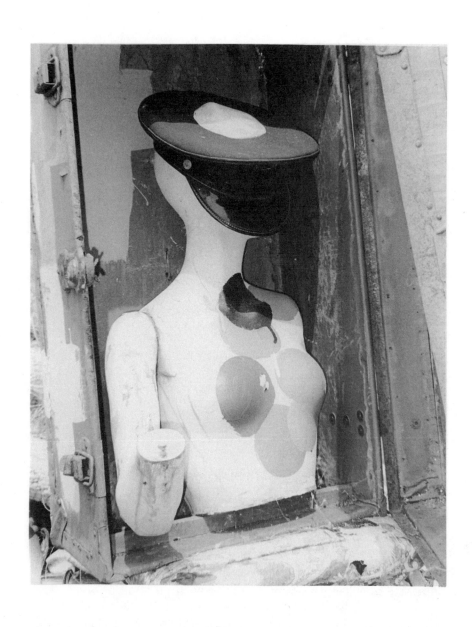

"My Life Undercover" from The Heidelberg Project,
photo by Sonya Badger, 1997.

Last Days of a Life Under Cover

Donna Stubak

Photo © Sonya Badger

Last Days of a Life Under Cover

When I finally weasel my way out from the woolly depths of my man's Appalachian hand-loomed blanket and breathe fresh air once again, it is plain as the nose on my face—what I am looking for isn't under there, after all. There is no love at all under there, just some stale cracker crumbs and a few pieces of moldy cheese.

I hid in the folds of that blanket, played tents, hide-n-seek and other games for too many years, counted red and yellow and green stripes. It was way too dark under there to tell a weasel from a man anyway. It's hard to find anything in the dark, let alone anything worthwhile. Sometimes I even tried to sing, to keep myself company, but the blanket muffled my voice. Still, I thought the cover of darkness lent a glamorous edge to plain old me.

To find a way out from under the cover, I decode a trail of cracker crumbs and colorful blanket fibers that look like letters of the alphabet. The letters begin to form words that at first seem cryptic, until I remember they are messages from my past, missing pieces of myself, that form a trail into the open.

Riding Shotgun for the Ragman

Donna Stubak

I am the Ragman's child, bought at a bargain price one Saturday morning so long ago, a Saturday like all others, that finds me playing in the space between the trash cans and the alley. I build castles in my sandbox that overlooks the alley gate. The landlord in the upstairs flat moved the sandbox in between the trash cans and the alley because he didn't want sand in his rose garden. The waiting time in the in-between space is finally over, so I scramble atop the rickety wagon and stand tall at the crest of a heap of discards: a bright collage of toys and clothes and old blankets. I don an eye patch and matching calico kerchief, scavenge a stained, white Communion dress from the rag pile and stand, steady and proud, at the helm of the Ragman's ship.

I ride shotgun for the Ragman, a dark, bent figure who holds the reins to an old, brown mare. The mare clomps patiently down the alleys, accepts apples and sugar cubes from the children who want to ride with the Ragman. She wears an old straw hat and a necklace of brass bells that tinkle as we ride. The Ragman has a brass horn that he blows. It calls to the children with a mournful wail. I ride shotgun and call out to the other hopeless children who wait in the in-between space. They wait to leave tiny square yards and trash cans and begin the ride that will show them the view from behind.

Their small hunched figures are delicately screened from the houses by perfumed wisteria vines, snowball bushes covered with puffy white pompoms and bright red trumpet vines that answer the wailing call of the Ragman's horn.

The wagon is becoming heavy with children. It settles in the rut that runs down the middle of the alley, an asphalt valley with gray-black hills that rise on each side. Dull orange brick buildings curve over us. We ride behind Sweetland's, and I taste fizzy sour strawberry sodas. Then we pass Kozak's Meat Market, and the odor of spoiled meat fills the air. The scent of buttery popcorn and musty velvet draperies wafts out from behind Martha Washington Theater. I taste Jujubes, Slo-pokes, and Sno-caps. An orange glow rises over the Martha Washington Bakery next door. Pinkish-orange neon hearts illuminate lacy wedding cakes in the front window. But in the alley, all that remain are crusts of moldy bread and cake crumbs.

The middle of the alley smells like the midway of a carnival—musky popcorn, cotton candy and sweaty old men. I call out to see who's going to ride with me and the Rag-man, "Cin-dee, Cin-dee, Gar-ee, Gar-ee, Jo-ee, Jo-ee."

The old men outside Kosciousko Bar sit around in shiny sharkskin suits and suspenders, read the *Dzienik Polske* and press dimes into the palms of little girls in the alley. They smell like Boilermakers and their suits shine silver-blue and green. They hawk, and spit and pee against the back of the building, wellaware they are being watched.

I move along to the plodding rhythm of the mare's steps. I see Madeleine on the back porch of her flat. She sits on a broken-down vinyl sofa, holds a brown bottle. Her face is a deflated balloon, her mouth a bright watermelon gash. Her hair, teased out to there, is a scary shade of orange. She's too old for the Ragman, so we pass her with a wave.

The alley continues to lie ahead, a long snake with pebbly gray skin. Its body writhes endlessly toward the horizon. How much more can I take? I'd like to hammer my sand castles into magic dust, sprinkle it on myself and fly home, but home is always the alley, my view always from behind.

"Waiting for the Ragman," by Sonya Badger, 1997, from The Heidelberg Project.

"Childhood Crucifixion," by Sonya Badger, 1997, from The Heidelberg Project"

The Crucifixion of Rabbit

Donna Stubak

Sunday night ritual
after pot roast dinner
eaten off the ceiling,
dessert of broken TV antennas
and tapioca:
little sister's re-enactment
of a scarcely noticed nighttime
drama, it's real hard to remember,
nights I covered heating vents.
Small and shivering,
I let the blast of hot air
lull me or curled into
the stinging mothball smell
of the hall closet, befriended the dark inside.

Sundays after church
and hymns, we played house till we tired
of Baby Bright. Then she, the director
with eyebrow-pencil mustache,
created a passion play, and I,
the captive audience, watched
the ritual execution of Rabbit,
raggedy fuzz-ball pink, from Easters
long ago. Rabbit was killed with high drama
on the living-room stage, then nailed
to a Popsicle stick cross. We watched his ears
droop, his stuffing slowly bleed out,
then dabbed his wounds with Mercurochrome.
His insides were outside now. We stuffed it all
back in, then added a few stitches
to hold him together till the next Sunday,
when we'd all reopen the wounds.

Donna Stubak

Fuzzy White Edges

I was afraid when it first happened,
when I first began to feel myself go away.
I looked at the white walls
after my dentist gave me
the shot that's supposed to keep the pain
away, and felt myself begin to disappear
around the edges. I wanted it
to stop. I screamed for a mirror, for someone
to tell me I was still there. I looked
everywhere for a reflection:
in the shiny metal spit bowl,
on the tray of sharp and mean
instruments, even in the tiny
tooth mirror. But that just showed
one round piece of me.

I blinked up
at the bright white eye,
breathed white walls, reached
under my white paper bib and held
my little wishing doll. He had
an ugly troll face and lots of wild
pink hair, streaked with purple, soft
and neon-bright. I used to rub
it and wish things would get better.

I touched purple, wished for white,
wished to let white, fuzzy edges move in closer,
softly replace all things lost until
my heartbeat muffled: *Quiet-quiet-white-white—*
while a wad of cotton in my mouth replaced the lost
tooth. I avoided the holes left, pulled down
white window shade walls and curled up

inside a fake gold chest beside my baby tooth.
I nestled into fuzzy white cotton, closed
the latch and tried to hide
from my roots.

Donna Stubak

Petey-bird

I forget the first part,
when Da held Petey-bird's throat
and twisted
real quick,
went back to his cigarettes, beer and TV.

I didn't want to look
at the bottom of the cage,
so I squinted my eyes before,
saw a blue-green blur.

Momma sprinkled holy water on Petey-bird,
gave me her rosary.
I counted off pearl bead prayers.
We recited,
Hail Mary, full of grace
Momma heard Da call,
turned away.
I counted off another prayer,
Our Father who art in heaven

I heard something break . . .
Thy kingdom come

I didn't want to touch Petey-bird, so
I put my winter mittens on,
lifted him, carried him
into the backyard and started digging,

dug until the shovel broke
and the hole was big
enough for Petey-bird
and me.

Donna Stubak

Tap Dancin' for Rita Bell at the Red House Chinese Restaurant

Finally! My big debut: the audition for Starlit Stairway's Silver Tap Award. Everyone is too hungry to wait for Hollywood, so we stop at the Red House Chinese Restaurant. The judges say their moo shoo shrimp is pretty good. As I sip my *cocktail*, a Shirley Temple (with a little pink and white paper umbrella), I see Little Richard at the piano, wearing a T-shirt with his picture on it. He starts playing *Blue Suede Shoes* and I'm hooked—I'm channeling Shirley Temple in her big dance scene in *The Little Princess*. The bartender lifts me up onto the gold marble bar, then straightens the white bows on my black patent tap shoes. Well, my feet work way past the shuffle-hop time steps taught to me by Miss Nancy. I catch the eye of the show's host, Rita Bell, and she gives me a big *thumbs up* sign.

I know I've never looked better (I wonder if Grampy notices). My costume, borrowed from my sister's Patti Playpal doll, is really really short, and the skirt flares out because it has this itch-stiff netting underneath and it's my favorite color, lavender satin with white feather trim and has spaghetti straps that bare my shoulders. I look older, at least thirteen. Also because I'm wearing Revlon's Forbidden Pink lipstick and blackest black mascara and liner. I see the way they look up at me. I throw my arms in the air and do the splits, all the way, for my grand finale, but it is very late and I'm suddenly limp. The final audition is coming up.

So Grampy drives me back to my room at the Hide-a-way Motel nearby. On the way back I press myself against the car door and notice a crack in the windshield that looks like a star. I think hard about that star, 'cause when I look out the window, the fire hydrants we pass are all crouched down low, and ready to pounce, like those flying monkeys from *The Wizard of Oz*, plus every piece of garbage looks like the body of an ol' dead dog.

Back at the Hide-a-way, I can't sleep—I keep waiting for the crickets to stop singing and the birds to start. I dream I feel Grampy's shadow pressed over me. I smell Jack Daniels and it's hard to breathe, so I think I wake up and hear the familiar clickety-smack-clack of Miss Nancy's high-heeled, silver tap shoes practicing time steps in the other room. A voice whispers that it's only the neighbors playing horseshoes, the clink of a ringer. Then I dream that I'm back up on the bar; I'm pelted with bags of Better Made chips, chocolate gold coins, and egg rolls, and I take off my costume and slip an egg roll under my head for a pillow. I dream I am in my Shirley Temple drink, under the pink and white umbrella, and I am sinking. I reach up to the maraschino cherries that float at the top, like red balloons, their stems just out of reach.

Donna Stubak

The Revolving Door

I push through the revolving door of Federal's Department Store. Although it's usually a simple in-and-out ride, today I'm really stuck inside, during the Day After Christmas Sale. Even though I like corners, and I have three to look at in here, today I am afraid. I feel myself curl up tight, like a kitten, fit myself into one of the corners. I pretend I'm in another corner, my favorite corner, under the Christmas tree. I mash down dough balls of Wonder bread and bake them on hot, colorful Christmas tree lights. I smoosh my face against the cold glass door. I want this ride to be over. But the harder I push, the more I stay stuck. I feel the department store in a somewhere space ahead of me, and I am so alone. I hear an echoing sound, a familiar voice in the distance. I think it's the voice of one of the Minders. I hear *own* and *sale* and other words that dart around in this three-cornered space. Minders like sales, they like to own things, they like to be liked, and mostly, they like to *have* people.

I try to pretend myself away from the Minders, so I am on my very favorite ride, seated between the pastel swans on the carousel at the fair. One swan is pink and the other is mint green. I want to move forward, but I still feel stuck. I look at the mint green swan. He returns my look with a small, black eye that shines red. Then I feel long feathers from each side envelop and lift me. I wrap myself up tight in a scarf of parking lot pebbles and bumper-guard strength and trail a plume of yellow fumes as the swans, with eyes that glow like red headlights, lift me above the revolving door. I look down and see the other stuck shoppers, pie-wedge prisoners. The harder they push forward, the more they move back. Uplifted and outstretched arms and hands move through glass barriers. From up here, the revolving door looks like a clock with hands that move back, each pie wedge a piece of time. Everyone moves so fast that I see what looks like a giant spinning top, dark green with sparks of red and yellow. The whirling top grows taller, into a towering Christmas tree.

The pale green swan gives me a dark, red look and drops me. I am caught on a top branch. I hang high and heavy there—a shiny, round, red Christmas ornament. A globe of blood. I reflect everything below like a fun-house mirror. Everything below is all red, too. I wonder if it just looks that way because I am red. I reflect and see everything. The streets run narrow and black, like so many alleys with tall buildings on each side. I suddenly feel glad that I hang high on the tree, hidden in the back—because, up here, I am safe from the Minders that live here in Otherville. The Minders pretend to live in the tall houses, but they really love alleys and low places best, and they have dark, bonnet eyes that pretend to be kind. They pretend to care for me, *mind* me—they pretend to take the place of the grandmothers I never knew and grandfathers I wish I never knew.

Like Ponee, next door, a neighborhood Minder—I see her through the hole in the knotty pine. She sits on her glider, on the porch next door, in a baggy, gray slip. Her breasts sag out of the slip, move in a loose rhythm that matches the motion of the glider.

Her wrinkled face and gray hair blend together. From inside the folds, her eyes peer out, sharp and dark, like the eyes of a rat. Her dark stare makes me feel quite heavy and rotten, like some of the overripe Christmas fruit I see at the bottom of the tree: tangerines, cactus peas, starfruit and pomegranates.

I am a blushing, full pomegranate, too heavy for a pine branch, so I fall down long and hard, split wide open, scatter shiny wet red kernels in all the redness that is already down there. I wonder if the Minders will come, drawn by the jewel-like color and scent. If they will nibble blood-red kernels scattered over sheep, donkeys and wise men, scattered among empty packages, festive ribbon and fake snow. If they will taste each seed with an appetite for a fresh and innocent universe, pierce sharp teeth through thin and tender skin, tear through bitter connecting membrane, into salty sweet juice, until all that is left is the hard, bitter seed at the core and pomegranate juice stain is everywhere—stain that seeps into every safe corner, into and over anyone curled up in the corner like a kitten, holding a tiny statue of the baby Jesus with broken feet that are stained, too.

Playing Chicken

Bad boy Phil Clark from public school whispers, "Wanna play a better game?" in my ear as we play red-light, green-light in the alley behind my house in Hamtramck. "Wanna play chicken?" Phil is my eleven-year-old Mick Jagger (though sister Karen says he looks somewhere between Pruneface from Dick Tracy comics and Edward G. Robinson). Sister Clarentia, my sixth-grade teacher at St. Ladislaus, always smacks me a good one with her special paddle with holes when I oogle at Phil on the days he skips school and passes St. Lad's. His Beatle boots are as black and pointy as the pencils I sharpen just to look out the window and watch him strut down Joseph Campau—tight tight jeans, black leather jacket with at least six zippers. He defiantly blows smoke rings toward Sister Clarentia's pinched face. She clutches her crucifix, looks at my pink cheeks and gives me the bad angel stamp on my behavior card.

Yes, I want to play a better game with Phil, so I meet him after school the next day on the playground between the church and St. Lad's School, under the monkey bars. I'm not surprised that my best friends—Diane Grabowski, Geneva Little and Lynn Pakulak— are there in front of the teeter-totters. They stand in a tight little row: six red kneesocks, three red-plaid pleated skirts, and three red berets stabbed into place at jaunty angles with three butterfly hatpins. "Debbie sends her best," they chorus cheerfully to me. They mean Debbie Patton, my other best friend. She can't be here, I know, because she is currently encased from neck to waist in a plaster cast to correct a spine problem. She is my very best friend, and she is the only other girl besides me, in sixth grade, who has her period and big breasts. Although she was held back two times. Still, I don't think she helped spread the rumor that I stuff my bra, after I graduated too soon from training bras into the adult ABC's of bradom.

"Are you chicken, are you for real?" Di chants. They all three look at me. Phil glances at them with a smooth, lidded look that slides over their red-plaid chests, and they look down at the flat-as-a-board expanse, then look at me again. Phil, under the monkey bars with me now, explains the rules I already know. He says he'll go slow, start low, go higher if I say to go, if I'm not chicken. I look through the monkey bars at the distant traffic light on Joseph Campau. Red light, stop—green light, go. Geneva turns up her transistor radio. Iron Butterfly sings, *In the garden of Eden, baby, don't you know that I love you . . .* I look through the monkey bars at the statue of Virgin Mary on the church lawn, and she gives me a cold marble stare. I feel my little Playtex butterfly nestled between my 34B's. Phil's hand reaches toward the butterfly, starts to unfasten buttons.

Through the monkey bars, I see Sister Clarentia come out of St. Lad's. Her long, coarse, black veil is blown up and away by the wind; then it floats away, like a big black bird, and she is left between the church and the school—exposed. She is white now, her head and neck covered by a tight, white hood with an endless row of tiny buttons that start at her back shoulder blades and end at her brow. I watch as she bows her head and begins unbuttoning. But then I realize she has dropped her spectacles and she's wildly fumbling for her veil. She can't see that her veil has blown toward me. Its shadow hovers, then lands almost on top of my three best friends. They split so fast that the dust of the playground is not even stirred. But not before they see that I'm not chicken. Phil runs too, before I feel the warmth of his hand seep through my Playtex lace. And I am alone. I button quickly, then run all the way home. I figure Sister Clarentia can't see me without her glasses.

I run straight to my bedroom, lock the door and sit for a minute, trying to catch my breath. I look at myself in the mirror and consider whether I feel different now. I unbutton my blouse, take off my bra. I wonder if I look sexy. I almost expect to see fingerprints on my breasts. Then I put on an old sweatshirt and do my homework.

Next morning, at school, there's a note taped on my locker that says, "To the slut." Inside I read, "Heard about last night. What do you think you proved? Why don't you ask your friends who started the rumor anyway? And ask them what the new rumor will be." It is unsigned, but looks like Geneva's writing.

During religious study period, after lunch, I sit behind Geneva and stare at the back of her blonde head. And think about how weird she's acting today. Ouch! Suddenly I feel a sharp pain in my left breast, by my heart. I look down and stuck to my plaid jumper is a pink wad of Bazooka Joe gum with a straight pin sticking out, like a tiny spear. I pull it off and throw it on the floor, under Geneva's desk. Then I look around. Three rows across, I see Geneva's steady, Mark Jaworski, altar boy/jock, look sideways at me and then pass a note to me. "How about stopping by Lou's garage tonight? Party starts about seven, and Geneva won't be there." I smile across the room at Mark and nod my head.

Mark asks me if I want a beer when I arrive, and I ask for a Bud, as if I know what I'm doing. Then I sit on the old couch next to Mark and ask him what kind of music he has. He says he hopes I like what he's got. The music of "Light My Fire" pours over me as I slam a beer down, then another. I relax enough to notice that Mark isn't even pretending to make eye contact, unless he thinks my nipples are eyes. He stares boldly at my breasts, outlined nicely in a tight-ribbed poor boy sweater. Then he kisses me. I look past him, at our reflection in the window, as he puts his hands under my shirt. He pulls my sweater off, then reaches around to unfasten my bra. I continue to watch our reflection. I tell Mark to wait and shotgun the rest of his beer. My breasts feel as heavy as two wet sandbags plastered over my ribs. I want to rip them off and throw them away, far away. I slam another beer, then let Mark take off my bra and touch my bare, shivering skin.

Donna Stubak

Tea Time

Daddy dear sent me a gift:
a blue and white punch pot,
matches my set of Willow Ware.
How very thoughtful to send
a gift that matches my dishes,
matches me. It's shaped like a lifesaver
with a perfectly round hole in the middle
like mine. The white porcelain skin
is etched with blue crosses,
forget-me-nots and arrows that trace
deeper pathways.

I serve Plain View Tea to the others on the Planning
Ideas Into Octagons Committee. I watch them through
the hole in the middle of the punch pot as I pour.
(Are they looking through my hole in the middle?)
They politely sip their tea.
I could say it came in handy
those past years when I was thrown
out to sea, had to float, and wait. Contemplate
forget-me-nots.

They just drink the good tea,
flavored with the oil of seven coriander seeds.
The first pressing, virgin pure and most potent. They
drink the tea, and I do, too.
I drink and drink, roll the pungent, grassy taste
of coriander in my mouth. Tell the committee how I fit
my ideas into octagons. (Do they like the way
I fit ideas into all the corners?) Suddenly
the smell of coffee, black, pushes
the fragrance of coriander away. And I hear Daddy say,
Pour me some coffee, you know I don't like tea,

and why use octagons when we've always used
squares at home—four-cornered and dependable, they used to
be good enough for you. Daddy, I reply, We are drinking
tea here, would you care for a cup?—

I am poised, ready to pour, look straight
through the hole in the pot, offer him a donut hole. He throws
the hole at me, it flies
through the middle of me,
lands at the feet of Mew Mew, my Siamese cat.
Oh my, does that hurt? Mew Mew asks, as she bats
the hole with a creamy paw. Her earrings dance against
her shapely head; cornflower blue sapphires pierce through
black velvet. *Your earrings match your eyes,*
but do the holes hurt? I ask.
Of course not, but at first they did, when the holes
were just made.

Exactly, I say.

Mom Makes Production on the Midnight Shift

She steps up to her pedestal place on Press #1, the draw, higher than almost everything, and close to the factory sky crossed with steel beams, and she begins—begins to play the huge press like an organ, slings steel back and forth. She moves into the sounds, the up and down pull, slings long, jagged-edged steel pieces into the draw, feels a thin, sparkly spray of dope that is there to soothe, lube, fill in weak spots, any fissure that wants to explode instead of expand.

KA-CHOOM. KA-CHOOM. The machine slams down ferociously, the factory floor heaves and buckles, pulls her down, then up again. She works the machine, plays it with sliding snake-tong arms that explore the metal inside the hot metal nest, feels its readiness for her expansion into and inside.

She feels the hairline cracks, flaws deep inside of her, lets her own sweat and the dope fill all those crevices and moves into the nest, spreads out, lets herself be re-formed, fender strong, then conveyed to Press #2 where metal jaws snip off her hangnail edges, and the excess trim, small and heavy, falls down of its own weight into the scrap chute: pieces of a blue ruffled bandanna, a smashed lipstick, a tampon and half a mother's ring, with crushed stones of peridot, sapphire and aquamarine.

KA-CHOOM. KA-CHOOM. The press opens and closes. She watches the guy on the hi-lo jack-off, KA-CHOOM, KA-CHOOM, to the rhythm of the pounding machines. As the sound continues to pull down, she works steadily to remake herself, make production, until very little is left and she is light enough to float above the factory floor. Each minute of her five-minute break, she smokes, inhales, picks flecks of tobacco off her lips, and surveys a neat stack of the essential parts of herself that she'll save against a time when she can no longer keep up.

Donna Stubak

Little Elevations

Forty hours before I turn forty, I turn into the crypt keeper, cackling, screeching, playing pinochle to pass the time with my cronies (I don't get a lot of meld, mostly marriages and half-pinochles, but I bid recklessly anyway), and I try not to mind the smell down here in the catacombs, where I age. I count the bones of dead Christians, put them into *like* and *don't like* piles and hope for more meld, a better hand next time.

Forty minutes before I turn forty, I become a Hawaiian Sacrificial Maiden, chanting the old Hawaiian prayer chant, the *Kumilipo*, that means *beginning in deep darkness*. My dive into the active volcano, Point Pelee, is serendipitous because, as I jump, the forty beads around my right ankle are caught on a ledge inside the mountain. The ledge is the lip of a little cave. It is a good place to wait for a while. It contains a cape of crimson feathers lined with red handkerchiefs and a few bottles of Captain Morgan's Spiced Rum. After I settle into the bottom of the volcano, I have two children with a burly construction worker named Joe who smokes cheap cigars and has hair on his back. We have two groundhogs, Ferlin and Gerta. Every night I read to them by the light of our lava lamp. Our favorites are: Theodore Roethke's *In a Dark Time* and Sylvia Plath's *Lady Lazarus*.

Forty seconds before I turn forty, I ask Ferlin to burrow to the surface to see if his shadow falls on a sheet of ice. I wait impatiently for his return, try to kill time by making mid-life lists: half-way, half-baked, half-a-man, half-alive, half-dead. Ferlin interrupts my list-making. He's back with a groundhog grin and good news!

Ferlin gestures excitedly with his glossy brown paws and says, "The old neighborhood has crumbled into ice cubes, the whole valley of Detroit is iced over. But I found a small community of groundhogs that have taken to living at slightly higher elevations in a nearby area. They form a circle every night and sing special groundhog songs that generate a lot of heat and melt the surrounding ice."

I look at Ferlin and, without hesitation, say, "Let's go!"
Ferlin turns and tunnels toward the surface, while I hold trustingly
to his soft tail, through the black tunnel. We reach the surface, just
as I turn forty.

Donna Stubak

Rose Monday

Rose sat up straight and began to really listen to Pastor Del during his sermon, instead of just pretending to listen. "This Monday, the day before Fat Tuesday and Ash Wednesday, is Rose Monday. Rose Monday is a day to wish for the roses of your fancy." Rose felt he looked right at her while he spoke. She knew he meant to say, "Rose Isabella Connelly, you may finally give voice to your dreams." Rose took a deep breath after she left the church. She was reminded of the way the air always smelled after she blew out her birthday candles. She felt the signs were all in place.

She made the Sign of the Cross, in the name of the Father, Son and Holy Spirit, as she prayed for her roses that night. But, even as she prayed and thought about the Holy Trinity, she realized that the sign of threes was her problem. Things always happen in threes: births, deaths, luck . . . anyhow, that was what her mother said, and that was just the way things went—like right after Uncle Oscar died, Cousin Millie from West Virginia got hit by a car. Then their little mutt, Pupsy, got parvo and died. Rose knew her luck came in threes, and it was even worse than all of that. Particularly relationships. Bad relationships. Bad love had always come to her in threes. All the men she had loved were either Jim or Dave or Rick.

Her ex-husband was Dave. He was a factory worker, just like her father, who was also named Dave. She stayed married for a long, long time, somehow because she thought she was supposed to—that there were no alternatives. Rose almost lost herself, pretending. She started to forget what was real for her. Still, after her divorce, Rose continued to stay stuck in the threes.

Rose preferred men who seemed beneath her. Like one of the Jims. He was practically illiterate. About all they had in common were sports teams (especially the Pistons) and sex. Then when he dumped her, she felt so low—lower than low, because an idiot had dumped her. Her most recent and current man, Rick, was married—very unhappily, or so he said. He told her he loved her, though, and she needed to hear it.

Nonetheless, she prayed hard for normal, good love—that was her wish, the rose of her fancy, the only thing that mattered, the only thing that seemed to always elude her. Her relationship with Rick gave her some small comfort, partly because she knew from experience not to expect too much. Rick gave her little loans sometimes too and, though she really needed the money, she felt he paid for a performance. He needed to feel *one up*. Rose could relate. Overall, things were going fairly well, until the dreams began, and sometimes she had to draw away from Rick's touch—little moments when his hands were spiders tickling her thighs and trying to get inside her underwear.

Spiders and roses. Her grandfather's rose garden. Her dreams became nightmares more and more frequently after Rick spent the night. But she never told Rick about the dreams. The last time he spent the night and they made love, she had the dream. She was very small, about four years old, playing in the grass by Grandfather's garden of roses. In her dream, it was a beautiful summer day and all around her it looked peaceful and beautiful. The roses smelled sweet, the birds sang merrily. Yet she was terrified, felt smothered by the smell of roses, felt unable to move, as if a huge weight pressed her to the ground. And the tickling of something, like spiders up her legs, up her underpants. She felt a familiar presence and smelled a familiar smell that made her feel dizzy with apprehension. She woke up sweating, not wanting to remember the dream. Rose would push the dream away each time she had it, just let it fade as quickly as possible. After those nights, she was glad to go to work at Lincoln Elementary. She loved being a kindergarten teacher. And she loved being with the innocent, trusting children. They loved her all the time, even if she didn't deserve it.

Rose was glad Rick had been understanding about her *moods*, as he called them. He was coming over tonight, and he even had a surprise for her. Rose wondered what it could be—Rick wasn't inclined, by his nature, to surprises. He was usually pretty predictable, a careful and thorough man in all ways. He was a fairly successful accountant. Sometimes she wondered why they were having this affair—didn't it upset the careful, cautious balance of his life?

Rose prepared carefully for their date. She was excited because it was the night before Rose Monday, and she couldn't figure what Rick's surprise could be. After her bath, Rose smoothed on her special lotion, a mixture she made with essential oils that were supposed to attract and enhance love: Jasmine, Rose Absolute, and a touch of Sandalwood. She called it Eros, after the god of love. She wondered how things would work out with Rick. But he was Rick number 3 and, so far, the third had not been a charm. She stayed stuck. But there were times she tried to break out of this cycle.

She remembered Hans. Hans had been a sensitive man. He'd published a book of poetry, some of it quite good. He had even written her a poem. Hans had introduced her to some wonderful artists and poets, like Charles Bukowski. She still had the book he'd given her by Bukowski called, *Love is a Dog From Hell*. She had appreciated his taste and thought they might have been falling in love. Eventually, he'd invited her to a very nice German restaurant to meet some of his friends. She'd overheard his friend Bob say, "She's great, I love her, so pretty too," when she'd returned from the ladies' room. They'd all drunk a lot of Liebfraumilch that night, and things had been going rather well, until she'd tried to eat her spaetzel. She'd been very nervous and wolfed it, then choked until the tears had run down her face and ruined her carefully-applied makeup. Even after she'd stopped choking her voice hadn't come back, only the littlest whisper had come out. She never did find her voice again that night. She'd been totally humiliated and seen it as a sign not to try to break out, ever again.

She heard the doorbell ring. It must be Rick. Rose greeted him with a long kiss. "Well, hello, that's the way I like to be greeted," he said as he handed her a dozen long-stemmed red roses and a small, black velvet box. "Bring out the champagne because tonight we're going to celebrate." He poured a glass for her and whispered, "I didn't want to tell you in case something went wrong, but today my divorce is final. We can get married right away."

Rose first noticed that he didn't ask her, he told her. She also noticed that she didn't feel happy. She felt a little confused and surprised at herself. Rick seemed to take her silence for agreement and kissed her passionately. He led her to the bedroom and started to take off her clothes.

After he was finished and asleep, Rose drifted off, too, and began to dream. She was again in the rose garden. She felt very

211

afraid. She realized she was not alone—there was someone above her. She thought it was a giant spider. Then she felt roses crush against her. They smelled too sweet and they scratched her with their thorns. She wondered about the giant spider. She felt him there, still. She smelled Old Spice, her grandfather's cologne. Then she was lying naked and he was over her, throwing roses on her naked body. The roses were blood-red and the petals were sharp, like razors. She held them against her arms, pressed their glittering, shiny edges against her skin. Red petals fell to the ground, became fluid, stained the floor with drops of red against white.

O

She woke up in the hospital, her arms swathed in white bandages. There was a vase of red roses from Rick on the nightstand. She turned away. Rose didn't feel grateful to Rick for saving her, forcing her to remember. She didn't want roses, didn't want Rick, didn't want to remember. She turned away and slept.

After she was discharged from the hospital, Rose lived slowly and carefully through the next days. The only things that gave her comfort and peace were sketching, painting and, sometimes, going to church. She liked to sketch the orchids at the Belle Isle Conservatory. The Easter flower display was wonderful this year. The air smelled sweet there, like warm earth. She especially loved a statue of a little girl holding a basin of water that splashed into a pool and was surrounded by hundreds of colorful orchids. When she sat before the little girl, she felt healing was possible.

On Easter Sunday, Rose sat in church surrounded by white Easter lilies. She began to sing along with everyone else and her voice rang out, loud and clear. She looked at the crucifix at the altar and thought about threes—how threes are like the Sign of the Cross: her past, her present and her future. "In the name of the Father," she touched her head, for her sad memories—then she touched her heart, "and of the Son," for feeling things here and now. She touched her right shoulder, then her left. "And of the Holy Spirit." The future. No more red roses.

About the Writers

Margo LaGattuta, editor, is a poet with four published books: *Embracing the Fall* (Plain View Press), *The Dream Givers* (Lake Shore Publishing), *Noedgelines* (Earhart Press) and *Diversion Road* (State Street Press). This is the third Michigan anthology she has edited for Plain View Press. The first, *Variations on the Ordinary*, was published in 1995, and the second, *Almost Touching*, was published in 1996. She co-edited and has poetry appearing in *Wind Eyes*, from Plain View Press in 1997. She has an MFA in Writing from Vermont College, teaches writing at Oakland Community College and hosts a weekly radio program. She is associate editor and columnist for *Suburban Lifestyles* newspaper and writes a monthly column for *Phenomenews*.

Kristin Palm is a freelance writer and editor, and a community education specialist for a community mental health program. She is a regular contributor to Detroit's news and arts weekly, the *Metro Times,* and an alum of *The Michigan Daily* at the University of Michigan, where she graduated with a BA in English. She began a master's program in Urban Planning at Wayne State University in the fall of 1997. She dedicates her work in this anthology to her sisters and mothers, in blood and in spirit, and especially to Mary Beauchamp Lane, whose strength, generosity, wit, will and wisdom have influenced her entire being.

Colleen Reader has received scholarships for the Cranbrook Writers' Conference and the National Writer's Voice Project. She has tenure in master-level poetry workshops with national award-winning poets Nick Bozanic, W.D. Ehrhart and Thomas Lynch. Reader, who lives and works in Milford, Michigan, was awarded first place honors by the Milford Fine Arts Association in 1997 for her poem *Abstract Art.*

Susan Paurazas was selected to participate in the 1996 Cranbrook Writers' Conference. She has attended Detroit Women Writers' Conferences at Oakland University and other writing seminars. She was editor and writer for *The Engineering and Science Newsletter* at the University of Detroit. Her work was published in a 1996 collection of essays called *Prism* dedicated to the prevention and awareness of violence against women. Paurazas is a dentist who is currently in a graduate specialty program. A wife and mother, she enjoys golf, aerobics, swimming, reading and traveling. This work is dedicated to her family members, especially her husband Fred and mother Beverly who have been a continual source of support and inspiration.

Denise Thomas has dabbled at writing for many years—journals, letters, and notebook paper filled with crabbed notes—but in 1994 she began in earnest to take time to write, to be obsessed with words and the page. She has had work published in *Speakeasy IV, V,* and *VI, A Wise Woman's Garden, Mind in Motion* and *Dream International Quarterly*. She has won honorable mention in Oakland Community College Woman Center's Our Vision competition for poetry and has been nominated for a Pushcart Prize for her short story "Chaos, Order, Moderation and a Spoon." Thomas is a founding member of the Clicking Bones Writers' Collective and contributes to that group's chapbook series. Her work also appears in the *Journal of the Magickal Education Council of Ann Arbor*.

Suzanne Dolan Manji is a visual artist and a psychiatric nurse in research. She has her own business, Alchemy, through which she creates custom assemblages based on individuals' lives. She combines her assemblages with poems and stories. She has exhibited her artwork in Virginia, Maryland, Washington D.C. and Michigan, where she currently lives. Manji's writing has appeared in *Washington Print Magazine, The Washington Flyer Magazine* and *Impulse Magazine*.

Nancy J. Henderson received her MA in Creative Writing from Antioch University in 1994. She has published her work in Plain View Press' *Variations on the Ordinary*, as well as in literary journals and chapbooks. She has also worked as an editor for a trade publication. Residing in a log home in Oxford, Michigan, she spends as much time as she can in the mountains of the Southwest and enjoys dancing and meditation.

Barbara Shooltz Kendzierski printed her first book of poetry at age seven for limited distribution (her parents). She has a degree in psychology and Spanish literature from Eastern Michigan University, where she was copy editor of *The Eastern Echo*. Kendzierski has a law degree from University of Michigan Law School and was senior editor of *The Michigan Law Review*. She practiced law for twelve years and edited an international newsletter on employee benefits law (where there was not much call for poetry). She lives in Troy, Michigan, with her husband and two sons.

Stephanie Matthews is a technical writer at Chrysler Corporation in Warren, Michigan. She graduated from Western Michigan University with a double English major—sharing emphases in both creative and technical writing. There she wrote articles for *The Western Herald*. Ever since she won a blue ribbon in second grade for her story "The Cross Carved Stone," Matthews has been drawn to writing. She has been published in literary magazines, including *Lunch*, *The Mustard Jar* and *Among Other Things*. Her favorite poets are Larry Levis and Elizabeth Bishop.

Donna Stubak, who works as assistant editor for *Singles Network Magazine*, has a BA in Journalism from Oakland University. When, as a child, she was asked what she wanted to be when she grew up, she answered, "A writer." She grew up in Hamtramck, Michigan, and enjoys writing about her old neighborhood, and about women in the factory. Writers who speak to her range from Sylvia Plath to Lewis Carroll.

Contributors' Notes

Kristin Palm:

More than writing what I know, I write what I want to know—my language, for instance. One of the great beauties of writing, and I think this is especially true with poetry, is that it fosters an intimate relationship between the writer and both her universal and personal tongues. In the universal sense, I am fascinated by the nuances of the English language, as well as my paternal grandmother's native Swedish—the way sounds and rhythms can evoke a particular tone, the effect of subtle but crucial differences in meaning, the magnificent impact of such a small thing as punctuation. In the personal sense, I redefine my language (and myself) every day. I consistently find myself exploring the language of connections—to things so obvious as family and friends, and so surprising as highways and cars; to things so nebular as the sun and the moon, and so mundane as lingerie and medicine. As I see (and hear) myself, I discover that I write and speak the language of women. It is not a conscious choice to explore this dialect. It is so much a part of who I am that it surfaces without my consciously calling upon it. This language must be understood as one that is not exclusive, but inclusive. It is a celebration of who and what I am—who and what we are—how we interact with one another and with the various elements of our selves and our earth. It is a language I write and speak in an effort to see myself—to see all of us—in our entirety.

Colleen Reader:

A seed pearl pin, polished stones on a satin cord, the ting of silver spoons, the wisdom in women's voices—to reclaim an engaging moment from oblivion is why I write poems. The musician in me strives for euphonic pleasures. The mathematician in me is drawn to the precision of language. My process of writing is more systematic than ethereal.

Susan Paurazas:

When I write, I share experience and feeling with snippets of words to create a visual picture. It is a way of bringing myself and the reader together, so that universal situations become personal and personal experiences expand to a common understanding. Writing is my attempt to create a landscape of feeling and thought using the limited tools of words and language. It makes the human experience spiritual and relates the spiritual in human, finite terms. By using concrete imagery to paint the landscape, I hope the reader sees the awe of a sunrise or sunset within his/her own mind, and with more imagination, beauty, and meaning than mere words can describe. This is where the magic lies.

Denise Thomas:

The world we live in measures and judges by a standard that ignores femaleness as anything but other, or deviant. Yes, much has changed in the past thirty years, but much has merely mutated and is less easily recognizable. How does this relate to my writing? How can it not? Whatever else I may be, believe, do, or know, I am still a womon. We all, each and every one on this planet, view the world and ourselves through the lens we have forged from our lives, a lens that is shaped by gender and culture. I write from my perspective, and my world is female.

Suzanne Dolan Manji:

When I was a child I asked serious questions. "What is it like to be married? How does it feel to be a teacher? Are you glad that you had children?" I am still asking the same questions. I'm consumed with relationships. Mother to child . . . man to woman . . . yellow to blue . . . figure to ground . . . chair to table . . . inside to outside . . . word to line. This is why I write . . . to put words next to each other and examine their relationships.

Nancy J. Henderson:

I find that the darkness of the soul, "duende," is strangely comforting to me. Like a flash of lightning, sometimes it enlightens me, beckons me to be real, to be human. I've never felt that the ideal in life was to be happy all the time or content or normal. My darkness makes me whole, gives me yang, balances my spirit. My writing is the voice of my spirit and puts me in balance with life.

Barbara Shooltz Kendzierski:

Some poems tumble onto the page and the best I can do is stand out of their way. Others wait patiently for me to understand. Some poems play coy, testing the depth of my commitment. I do not often know where the journey leads until the poem tells me we have arrived. The poem is a reminder—a reminder to honor the journey itself, to be awake to the unexpected, to grow with the unforeseen. Words are both my prison and my hope. I sometimes envy the dancer, the sculptor, the composer who can express layers of meaning in a language free of words. Yet always I am drawn back by the textures and rhythms of words—and by their power to reveal far more than what is written on the page. I find hope in the healing energy of poetry and the bridges it builds.

Stephanie Matthews:

The flame of the candle has purpose. I write to have purpose. Writing allows me to resolve conflict. After the storm I can analyze the aftermath; it gives me peace. Without words to express my confusion, I would be left with muddled thoughts. Writing dissolves space and time. My past becomes my present, which better equips me for the future—I know that if I were left with nothing, I could break apart the puzzle and analyze each piece. Writing is rediscovering myself. All the confusing turmoil of life is words tossed in the air. When they land into lines with feeling—only then does my life make sense.

Donna Stubak:

When my pen touches paper it connects me, makes me whole. All the parts of me—my spiritual self, my child self, my woman self—are integrated. Writing, for me, is a process of remembering. Just as I never knew my grandmothers, who both died by age thirty, I also never knew myself. I could not remember a painful past. Finally, pen in hand, I have a voice—a lovely voice. I speak for my grandmothers, my mother and myself.